P9-DFE-923

Under the Sign of Saturn

Under the Sign of Saturn

Susan Sontag

VINTAGE BOOKS
A DIVISION OF RANDOM HOUSE
NEW YORK

First Vintage Books Edition, October 1981
Copyright © 1972, 1973, 1975, 1976, 1978, 1980 by Susan Sontag
All rights reserved under International and Pan-American
Copyright Conventions. Published in the United States by Random
House, Inc., New York, and simultaneously in Canada by
Random House of Canada Limited, Toronto. Originally published by Farrar,
Straus & Giroux, New York, in 1980, and simultaneously in Canada
by McGraw-Hill, Ryerson Ltd., Toronto.

The New York Review of Books first published, in a somewhat different or
abridged form, "On Paul Goodman" in Vol. XIX, No. 4 (Sept. 21, 1972);
"Fascinating Fascism" in Vol. XXII, No. 1 (Feb. 6, 1975);
"Under the Sign of Saturn" in Vol. XXV, No. 15 (Oct. 12, 1978);
"Syberberg's Hitler" in Vol. XXVII, No. 2 (Feb. 21, 1980);
"Remembering Barthes" in Vol. XXVII, No. 8 (May 15, 1980);
and "Mind as Passion" in Vol. XXVII, No. 14 (Sept. 25, 1980).
"Approaching Artaud," written to introduce the Selected
Writings of Antonin Artaud (Farrar, Straus and Giroux, 1976)
which I edited, first appeared in The New Yorker, May 19, 1973.

I am grateful, as always, to Robert Silves for encouragement and
advice; and to Sharon DeLano for generous help in getting
several of the essays into final form.
S.S.

Library of Congress Cataloging in Publication Data
Sontag, Susan, 1933-
Under the sign of Saturn.
Reprint. Originally published: New York:
Farrar, Straus & Giroux, 1980.
Contents: On Paul Goodman—Approaching Artaud
—Fascinating Fascism—{etc.}
1. Arts, Modern—20th century. I. Title.
NX456.S58 1981 700'.9'04 81-40073
ISBN 0-394-74742-9 AACR2

Manufactured in the United States of America

FOR JOSEPH BRODSKY

Contents

Hamm: I love the old questions.
        (With fervour.)
        Ah the old questions, the old answers,
        there's nothing like them!
                                    Endgame

On Paul Goodman

I am writing this in a tiny room in Paris, sitting on a wicker chair at a typing table in front of a window which looks onto a garden; at my back is a cot and a night table; on the floor and under the table are manuscripts, notebooks, and two or three paperback books. That I have been living and working for more than a year in such small bare quarters, though not at the beginning planned or thought out, undoubtedly answers to some need to strip down, to close off for a while, to make a new start with as little as possible to fall back on. In this Paris in which I live now, which has as little to do with the Paris of today as the Paris of today has to do with the great Paris, capital of the nineteenth century and seedbed of art and ideas until the late 1960s, America is the closest of all the faraway places. Even during periods when I don't go out at all—and in the last months there have been many blessed days and nights when

I have no desire to leave the typewriter except to sleep—
each morning someone brings me the Paris *Herald Tribune*
with its monstrous collage of "news" of America, encapsu-
lated, distorted, stranger than ever from this distance: the
B-52s raining ecodeath on Vietnam, the repulsive martyrdom of Thomas Eagleton, the paranoia of Bobby Fischer,
the irresistible ascension of Woody Allen, excerpts from the
diary of Arthur Bremer—and, last week, the death of Paul
Goodman.

I find that I can't write just his first name. Of course, we
called each other Paul and Susan whenever we met, but
both in my head and in conversation with other people he
was never Paul or ever Goodman but always Paul Goodman—the whole name, with all the ambiguity of feeling
and familiarity which that usage implies.

The grief I feel at Paul Goodman's death is sharper because we were not friends, though we co-inhabited several
of the same worlds. We first met eighteen years ago. I was
twenty-one, a graduate student at Harvard, dreaming of
living in New York, and on a weekend trip to the city
someone I knew who was a friend of his brought me to the
loft on Twenty-third Street where Paul Goodman and his
wife were celebrating his birthday. He was drunk, he
boasted raucously to everyone about his sexual exploits, he
talked to me just long enough to be mildly rude. The second
time we met was four years later at a party on Riverside
Drive, where he seemed more subdued but just as cold and
self-absorbed.

In 1959 I moved to New York, and from then on
through the late 1960s we met often, though always in
public—at parties given by mutual friends, at panel discus-

sions and Vietnam teach-ins, on marches, in demonstrations. I usually made a shy effort to talk to him each time we met, hoping to be able to tell him, directly or indirectly, how much his books mattered to me and how much I had learned from him. Each time he rebuffed me and I retreated. I was told by mutual friends that he didn't really like women as people—though he made an exception for a few particular women, of course. I resisted that hypothesis as long as I could (it seemed to me cheap), then finally gave in. After all, I had sensed just that in his writings: for instance, the major defect of *Growing Up Absurd*, which purports to treat the problems of American youth, is that it talks about youth as if it consists only of adolescent boys and young men. My attitude when we met ceased being open.

Last year another mutual friend, Ivan Illich, invited me to Cuernavaca at the same time that Paul Goodman was there giving a seminar, and I told Ivan that I preferred to come after Paul Goodman had left. Ivan knew, through many conversations, how much I admired Paul Goodman's work. But the intense pleasure I felt each time at the thought that he was alive and well and writing in the United States of America made an ordeal out of every situation in which I actually found myself in the same room with him and sensed my inability to make the slightest contact with him. In that quite literal sense, then, not only were Paul Goodman and I not friends, but I disliked him— the reason being, as I often explained plaintively during his lifetime, that I felt he didn't like me. How pathetic and merely formal that dislike was I always knew. It is not Paul Goodman's death that has suddenly brought this home to me.

He had been a hero of mine for so long that I was not in the least surprised when he became famous and always a little surprised that people seemed to take him for granted. The first book of his I ever read—I was seventeen—was a collection of stories called *The Break-up of Our Camp*, published by New Directions. Within a year I had read everything he'd published, and from then on started keeping up. There is no living American writer for whom I have felt the same simple curiosity to read as quickly as possible *anything* he wrote, on any subject. That I mostly agreed with what he thought was not the main reason; there are other writers I agree with to whom I am not so loyal. It was that voice of his that seduced me—that direct, cranky, egotistical, generous American voice. If Norman Mailer is the most brilliant writer of his generation, it is surely by reason of the authority and eccentricity of his voice; and yet I for one have always found that voice too baroque, somehow fabricated. I admire Mailer as a writer, but I don't really believe in his voice. Paul Goodman's voice is the real thing. There has not been such a convincing, genuine, singular voice in our language since D. H. Lawrence. Paul Goodman's voice touched everything he wrote about with intensity, interest, and his own terribly appealing sureness and awkwardness. What he wrote was a nervy mixture of syntactical stiffness and verbal felicity; he was capable of writing sentences of a wonderful purity of style and vivacity of language, and also capable of writing so sloppily and clumsily that one imagined he must be doing it on purpose. But it never mattered. It was his voice, that is to say, his intelligence and the poetry of his intelligence incarnated, which kept me a loyal and passionate addict. Though he was not often graceful as a writer, his writing and his mind were touched with grace.

There is a terrible, mean American resentment toward a writer who tries to do many things. The fact that Paul Goodman wrote poetry and plays and novels as well as social criticism, that he wrote books on intellectual specialties guarded by academic and professional dragons, such as city planning, education, literary criticism, psychiatry, was held against him. His being an academic freeloader and an outlaw psychiatrist, while also being so smart about universities and human nature, outraged many people. That ingratitude is and always was astonishing to me. I know that Paul Goodman often complained of it. Perhaps the most poignant expression was in the journal he kept between 1955 and 1960, published as *Five Years*, in which he laments the fact that he is not famous, not recognized and rewarded for what he is.

That journal was written at the end of his long obscurity, for with the publication of *Growing Up Absurd* in 1960 he did become famous, and from then on his books had a wide circulation and, one imagines, were even widely read—if the extent to which Paul Goodman's ideas were repeated (without his being given credit) is any proof of being widely read. From 1960 on, he started making money as he was taken more seriously—and he was listened to by the young. All that seems to have pleased him, though he still complained that he was not famous enough, not read enough, not appreciated enough.

Far from being an egomaniac who could never get enough, Paul Goodman was quite right in thinking that he never had the attention he deserved. That comes out clearly enough in the obituaries I have read since his death in the half-dozen American newspapers and magazines that I get here in Paris. In these obituaries he is no more than that maverick interesting writer who spread himself too thin, who published *Growing Up Absurd*, who influenced the rebellious American youth of the 1960s, who was indiscreet about his sexual life. Ned Rorem's touching obituary, the only one I have read that gives any sense of Paul Goodman's importance, appeared in *The Village Voice*, a paper read by a large part of Paul Goodman's constituency, only on page 17. As the assessments come in now that he is dead, he is being treated as a marginal figure.

I would hardly have wished for Paul Goodman the kind of media stardom awarded to McLuhan or even Marcuse—which has little to do with actual influence and doesn't tell one anything about how much a writer is being read. What I am complaining about is that Paul Goodman was often taken for granted even by his admirers. It has never been clear to most people, I think, what an extraordinary figure he was. He could do almost anything, and tried to do almost everything a writer can do. Though his fiction became increasingly didactic and unpoetic, he continued to grow as a poet of considerable and entirely unfashionable sensibility; one day people will discover what good poetry he wrote. Most of what he said in his essays about people, cities, and the feel of life is true. His so-called amateurism is identical with his genius: that amateurism enabled him to bring to the questions of schooling, psychiatry, and citizenship an extraordinary, curmudgeonly accuracy of insight and freedom to envisage practical change.

It is difficult to name all the ways in which I feel indebted to him. For twenty years he has been to me quite simply the most important American writer. He was our Sartre, our Cocteau. He did not have the first-class theoretical intelligence of Sartre; he never touched the mad, opaque source of genuine fantasy that Cocteau had at his disposal in practicing so many arts. But he had gifts that neither Sartre nor Cocteau ever had: an intrepid feeling for what human life is about, a fastidiousness and breadth of moral passion. His voice on the printed page is real to me as the voices of few writers have ever been—familiar, endearing, exasperating. I suspect there was a nobler human being in his books than in his life, something that happens often in "literature." (Sometimes it is the other way around, and the person in real life is nobler than the person in the books. Sometimes there is hardly any relationship between the person in the books and the person in real life.)

I gained energy from reading Paul Goodman. He was one of that small company of writers, living and dead, who established for me the value of being a writer and from whose work I drew the standards by which I measured my own. There have been some living European writers in that diverse and very personal pantheon, but no living American writer apart from him. Everything he did on paper pleased me. I liked it when he was pigheaded, awkward, wistful, even wrong. His egotism touched me rather than put me off (as Mailer's often does when I read him). I admired his diligence, his willingness to serve. I admired his courage, which showed itself in so many ways—one of the most admirable being his honesty about his homosexuality in *Five Years*, for which he was much criticized by his straight friends in the New York intellectual world; that was six years ago, before the advent of Gay Liberation made coming out of the closet chic. I liked it when he talked about himself and when he mingled his own sad sexual desires with his desire for the polity. Like André Breton, to whom he could be compared in many ways, Paul Goodman was a connoisseur of freedom, joy, pleasure. I learned a great deal about those three things from reading him.

This morning, starting to write this, I reached under the table by the window to get some paper for the typewriter and saw that one of the three paperback books buried under the manuscripts is *New Reformation*. Although I am trying to live for a year without books, a few manage to creep in somehow. It seems fitting that even here, in this tiny room where books are forbidden, where I try better to hear my own voice and discover what I really think and really feel, there is still at least one book by Paul Goodman around, for there has not been an apartment in which I have lived for the last twenty-two years that has not contained most of his books.

With or without his books, I shall go on being marked by him. I shall go on grieving that he is no longer alive to talk in new books, and that now we all have to go on in our fumbling attempts to help each other and to say what is true and to release what poetry we have and to respect each other's madness and right to be wrong and to cultivate our sense of citizenliness without Paul's hectoring, without Paul's patient meandering explanations of everything, without the grace of Paul's example.

(1972)

Approaching Artaud

The movement to disestablish the "author" has been at work for over a hundred years. From the start, the impetus was—as it still is—apocalyptic: vivid with complaint and jubilation at the convulsive decay of old social orders, borne up by that worldwide sense of living through a revolutionary moment which continues to animate most moral and intellectual excellence. The attack on the "author" persists in full vigor, though the revolution either has not taken place or, wherever it did, has quickly stifled literary modernism. Gradually becoming, in those countries not recast by a revolution, the dominant tradition of high literary culture instead of its subversion, modernism continues to evolve codes for preserving the new moral energies while temporizing with them. That the historical imperative which appears to discredit the very practice of literature has lasted so long—a span covering numerous literary generations—does not mean that it was incorrectly understood. Nor does it mean that the malaise of the "author" has now become outmoded or inappropriate, as is sometimes suggested. (People tend to become cynical about even the most appalling crisis if it seems to be dragging on, failing to come to term.) But the longevity of modernism does show what happens when the prophesied resolution of drastic social and psychological anxiety is postponed—what unsuspected capacities for ingenuity and agony, and the domestication of agony, may flourish in the interim.

In the established conception under chronic challenge, literature is fashioned out of a rational—that is, socially accepted—language into a variety of internally consistent types of discourse (e.g., poem, play, epic, treatise, essay, novel) in the form of individual "works" that are judged by such norms as veracity, emotional power, subtlety, and relevance. But more than a century of literary modernism has made clear the contingency of once stable genres and undermined the very notion of an autonomous work. The standards used to appraise literary works now seem by no means self-evident, and a good deal less than universal. They are a particular culture's confirmations of its notions of rationality: that is, of mind and of community.

Being an "author" has been unmasked as a role that, whether conformist or not, remains inescapably responsible to a given social order. Certainly not all pre-modern authors flattered the societies in which they lived. One of the author's most ancient roles is to call the community to account for its hypocrisies and bad faith, as Juvenal in the *Satires* scored the follies of the Roman aristocracy, and Richardson in *Clarissa* denounced the bourgeois institution of property-marriage. But the range of alienation available to the pre-modern authors was still limited— whether they knew it or not—to castigating the values of one class or milieu on behalf of the values of another class or milieu. The modern authors are those who, seeking to escape this limitation, have joined in the grandiose task set forth by Nietzsche a century ago as the transvaluation of all values, and redefined by Antonin Artaud in the twentieth century as the "general devaluation of values." Quixotic as this task may be, it outlines the powerful strategy by which the modern authors declare themselves to be no longer responsible—responsible in the sense that authors who celebrate their age and authors who criticize it are equally citizens in good standing of the society in which they function. The modern authors can be recognized by their effort to disestablish themselves, by their will not to be morally useful to the community, by their inclination to present themselves not as social critics but as seers, spiritual adventurers, and social pariahs.

Inevitably, disestablishing the "author" brings about a redefinition of "writing." Once writing no longer *defines* itself as responsible, the seemingly common-sense distinction between the work and the person who produced it, between public and private utterance, becomes void. All pre-modern literature evolves from the classical conception of writing as an impersonal, self-sufficient, freestanding achievement. Modern literature projects a quite different idea: the romantic conception of writing as a medium in which a singular personality heroically exposes itself. This ultimately private reference of public, literary discourse does not require that the reader actually know a great deal about the author. Although ample biographical information is available about Baudelaire and next to nothing is known about the life of Lautréamont, *The Flowers of Evil* and *Maldoror* are equally dependent as literary works upon the idea of the author as a tormented self raping its own unique subjectivity.

In the view initiated by the romantic sensibility, what is produced by the artist (or the philosopher) contains as a regulating internal structure an account of the labors of subjectivity. Work derives its credentials from its place in a singular lived experience; it assumes an inexhaustible personal totality of which "the work" is a by-product, and inadequately expressive of that totality. Art becomes a statement of self-awareness—an awareness that presupposes a disharmony between the self of the artist and the community. Indeed, the artist's effort is measured by the size of its rupture with the collective voice (of "reason"). The artist is a consciousness trying to be. "I am he who, in order to be, must whip his innateness," writes Artaud—modern literature's most didactic and most uncompromising hero of self-exacerbation.

In principle, the project cannot succeed. Consciousness as given can never wholly constitute itself in art but must strain to transform its own boundaries and to alter the boundaries of art. Thus, any single "work" has a dual status. It is both a unique and specific and already enacted literary gesture, and a meta-literary declaration (often strident, sometimes ironic) about the insufficiency of literature with respect to an ideal condition of consciousness and art. Consciousness conceived of as a project creates a standard that inevitably condemns the "work" to be incomplete. On the model of the heroic consciousness that aims at nothing less than total self-appropriation, literature will aim at the "total book." Measured against the idea of the total book, all writing, in practice, consists of fragments. The standard of beginnings, middles, and ends no longer applies. Incompleteness becomes the reigning modality of art and thought, giving rise to anti-genres— work that is deliberately fragmentary or self-canceling, thought that undoes itself. But the successful overthrow of old standards does not require denying the failure of such art. As Cocteau says, "the only work which succeeds is that which fails."

The career of Antonin Artaud, one of the last great exemplars of the heroic period of literary modernism, starkly sums up these revaluations. Both in his work and in his life, Artaud failed. His work includes verse; prose poems; film scripts; writings on cinema, painting, and literature; essays, diatribes, and polemics on the theater; several plays, and notes for many unrealized theater projects, among them an opera; a historical novel; a four-part dramatic monologue written for radio; essays on the peyote cult of the Tarahumara Indians; radiant appearances in two great films (Gance's *Napoleon* and Dreyer's *The Passion of Joan of Arc*) and many minor ones; and hundreds of letters, his most accomplished "dramatic" form—all of which amount to a broken, self-multilated corpus, a vast collection of fragments. What he bequeathed was not achieved works of art but a singular presence, a poetics, an aesthetics of thought, a theology of culture, and a phenomenology of suffering.

In Artaud, the artist as seer crystallizes, for the first time, into the figure of the artist as pure victim of his consciousness. What is prefigured in Baudelaire's prose poetry of spleen and Rimbaud's record of a season in hell becomes Artaud's statement of his unremitting, agonizing awareness of the inadequacy of his own consciousness to itself—the torments of a sensibility that judges itself to be irreparably estranged from thought. Thinking and using language become a perpetual calvary.

The metaphors that Artaud uses to describe his intellectual distress treat the mind either as a property to which one never holds clear title (or whose title one has lost) or as a physical substance that is intransigent, fugitive, unstable, obscenely mutable. As early as 1921, at the age of twenty-five, he states his problem as that of never managing to possess his mind "in its *entirety*." Throughout the nineteen-twenties, he laments that his ideas "abandon" him, that he is unable to "discover" his ideas, that he cannot "attain" his mind, that he has "lost" his understanding of words and "forgotten" the forms of thought. In more direct metaphors, he rages against the chronic erosion of his ideas, the way his thought crumbles beneath him or leaks away; he describes his mind as fissured, deteriorating, petrifying, liquefying, coagulating, empty, impenetrably dense: words rot. Artaud suffers not from doubt as to whether his "I" thinks but from a conviction that he does not possess his own thought. He does not say that he is unable to think; he says that he does not "have" thought— which he takes to be much more than having correct ideas or judgments. "Having thought" means that process by which thought sustains itself, manifests itself to itself, and is answerable "to all the circumstances of feeling and of life." It is in this sense of thought, which treats thought as both subject and object of itself, that Artaud claims not to "have" it. Artaud shows how the Hegelian, dramatistic, self-

regarding consciousness can reach the state of total alienation (instead of detached, comprehensive wisdom)—
because the mind remains an object.

The language that Artaud uses is profoundly contradic-
tory. His imagery is materialistic (making the mind into a
thing or object), but his demand on the mind amounts to
the purest philosophical idealism. He refuses to consider
consciousness except as a process. Yet it is the process character of consciousness—its unseizability and flux—that he
experiences as hell. "The real pain," says Artaud, "is to
feel one's thought shift within oneself." The *cogito*, whose
all too evident existence seems hardly in need of proof,
goes in desperate, inconsolable search of an *ars cogitandi*.
Intelligence, Artaud observes with horror, is the purest
contingency. At the antipodes of what Descartes and Valéry relate in their great optimistic epics about the quest
for clear and distinct ideas, a Divine Comedy of thought,
Artaud reports the unending misery and bafflement of consciousness seeking itself: "this intellectual tragedy in which
I am always vanquished," the Divine Tragedy of thought.
He describes himself as "in constant pursuit of my intellectual being."

The consequence of Artaud's verdict upon himself—his
conviction of his chronic alienation from his own consciousness—is that his mental deficit becomes, directly or
indirectly, the dominant, inexhaustible subject of his writings. Some of Artaud's accounts of his Passion of thought
are almost too painful to read. He elaborates little on his
emotions—panic, confusion, rage, dread. His gift was not
for psychological understanding (which, not being good at
it, he dismissed as trivial) but for a more original mode of
description, a kind of physiological phenomenology of

his unending desolation. Artaud's claim in *The Nerve Meter* that no one has ever so accurately charted his "intimate" self is not an exaggeration. Nowhere in the entire history of writing in the first person is there as tireless and detailed a record of the microstructure of mental pain.

Artaud does not simply record his psychic anguish, however. It constitutes his work, for while the act of writing—to give form to intelligence—is an agony, that agony also supplies the energy for the act of writing. Although Artaud was fiercely disappointed when the relatively shapely poems he submitted to the *Nouvelle Revue Française* in 1923 were rejected by its editor, Jacques Rivière, as lacking in coherence and harmony, Rivière's strictures proved to be liberating. From then on, Artaud denied that he was simply creating more art, adding to the storehouse of "literature." The contempt for literature—a theme of modernist literature first loudly sounded by Rimbaud—has a different inflection as Artaud expresses it in the era when the Futurists, Dadaists, and Surrealists had made it a commonplace. Artaud's contempt for literature has less to do with a diffuse nihilism about culture than with a specific experience of suffering. For Artaud, the extreme mental —and also physical—pain that feeds (and authenticates) the act of writing is necessarily falsified when that energy is transformed into artistry: when it attains the benign status of a finished, literary product. The verbal humiliation of literature ("All writing is garbage," Artaud declares in *The Nerve Meter*) safeguards the dangerous, quasimagical status of writing as a vessel worthy of bearing the author's pain. Insulting art (like insulting the audience) is an attempt to head off the corruption of art, the banalization of suffering.

The link between suffering and writing is one of Artaud's leading themes: one earns the right to speak through having suffered, but the necessity of using language is itself the central occasion for suffering. He describes himself as ravaged by a "stupefying confusion" of his "language in its relations with thought." Artaud's alienation from language presents the dark side of modern poetry's successful verbal alienations—of its creative use of language's purely formal possibilities and of the ambiguity of words and the artificiality of fixed meanings. Artaud's problem is not what language is in itself but the relation language has to what he calls "the intellectual apprehensions of the flesh." He can barely afford the traditional complaint of all the great mystics that words tend to petrify living thought and to turn the immediate, organic, sensory stuff of experience into something inert, merely verbal. Artaud's fight is only secondarily with the deadness of language; it is mainly with the refractoriness of his own inner life. Employed by a consciousness that defines itself as paroxysmic, words become knives. Artaud appears to have been afflicted with an extraordinary inner life, in which the intricacy and clamorous pitch of his physical sensations and the convulsive intuitions of his nervous system seemed permanently at odds with his ability to give them verbal form. This clash between facility and impotence, between extravagant verbal gifts and a sense of intellectual paralysis, is the psychodramatic plot of everything Artaud wrote; and to keep that contest dramatically valid calls for the repeated exorcising of the respectability attached to writing.

Thus, Artaud does not so much free writing as place it under permanent suspicion by treating it as the mirror of consciousness—so that the range of what can be written is made coextensive with consciousness itself, and the truth of any statement is made to depend on the vitality and wholeness of the consciousness in which it originates. Against all hierarchical, or Platonizing, theories of mind, which make one part of consciousness superior to another part, Artaud upholds the democracy of mental claims, the right of every level, tendency, and quality of the mind to be heard: "We can do anything in the mind, we can speak in any tone of voice, *even one that is unsuitable.*" Artaud refuses to exclude any perception as too trivial or crude. Art should be able to report from anywhere, he thinks—although not for the reasons that justify Whitmanesque openness or Joycean license. For Artaud, to bar any of the possible transactions between different levels of the mind and the flesh amounts to a dispossession of thought, a loss of vitality in the purest sense. That narrow tonal range which makes up "the so-called literary tone"—literature in its traditionally acceptable forms—becomes worse than a fraud and an instrument of intellectual repression. It is a sentence of mental death. Artaud's notion of truth stipulates an exact and delicate concordance between the mind's "animal" impulses and the highest operations of the intellect. It is this swift, wholly unified consciousness that Artaud invokes in the obsessive accounts of his own mental insufficiency and in his dismissal of "literature."

The quality of one's consciousness is Artaud's final standard. He unfailingly attaches his utopianism of consciousness to a psychological materialism: the absolute mind is also absolutely carnal. Thus, his intellectual distress is at the same time the most acute physical distress, and each statement he makes about his consciousness is also a statement about his body. Indeed, what causes Artaud's incurable pain of consciousness is precisely his refusal to consider the mind apart from the situation of the flesh. Far from being disembodied, his consciousness is one whose martyrdom results from its seamless relation to the body. In his struggle against all hierarchical or merely dualistic notions of consciousness, Artaud constantly treats his mind as if it *were* a kind of body—a body that he could not "possess," because it was either too virginal or too defiled, and also a mystical body by whose disorder he was "possessed."

It would be a mistake, of course, to take Artaud's statement of mental impotence at face value. The intellectual incapacity he describes hardly indicates the limits of his work (Artaud displays no inferiority in his powers of reasoning) but does explain his project: minutely to retrace the heavy, tangled fibers of his body-mind. The premise of Artaud's writing is his profound difficulty in matching "being" with hyperlucidity, flesh with words. Struggling to embody live thought, Artaud composed in feverish, irregular blocks; writing abruptly breaks off and then starts again. Any single "work" has a mixed form; for instance, between an expository text and an oneiric description he frequently inserts a letter—a letter to an imaginary correspondent or a real letter that omits the name of the addressee. Changing forms, he changes breath. Writing is conceived of as unleashing an unpredictable flow of searing energy; knowledge must explode in the reader's nerves. The details of Artaud's stylistics follow directly from his notion of consciousness as a morass of difficulty and suffering. His determination to crack the carapace of "literature"—at least, to violate the self-protective distance between reader and text—is scarcely a new ambition in the history of literary modernism. But Artaud may have come closer than any other author to actually doing it—by the violent discontinuity of his discourse, by the extremity of his emotion, by the purity of his moral purpose, by the excruciating carnality of the account he gives of his mental life, by the genuineness and grandeur of the ordeal he endured in order to use language at all.

The difficulties that Artaud laments persist because he is thinking about the unthinkable—about how body is mind and how mind is also a body. This inexhaustible paradox is mirrored in Artaud's wish to produce art that is at the same time anti-art. The latter paradox, however, is more hypothetical than real. Ignoring Artaud's disclaimers, readers will inevitably assimilate his strategies of discourse to art whenever those strategies reach (as they often do) a certain triumphant pitch of incandescence. And three small books published between 1925 and 1929—*The Umbilicus of Limbo*, *The Nerve Meter*, and *Art and Death*—which may be read as prose poems, more splendid than anything that Artaud did formally as a poet, show him to be the greatest prose poet in the French language since the Rimbaud of *Illuminations* and *A Season in Hell*. Yet it would be incorrect to separate what is most accomplished as literature from his other writings.

Artaud's work denies that there is any difference between art and thought, between poetry and truth. Despite the breaks in exposition and the varying of "forms" within each work, everything he wrote advances a line of argument. Artaud is always didactic. He never ceased insulting, complaining, exhorting, denouncing—even in the poetry written after he emerged from the insane asylum in Rodez, in 1946, in which language becomes partly unintelligible; that is, an unmediated physical presence. All his writing is in the first person, and is a mode of address in the mixed voices of incantation and discursive explanation. His activities are simultaneously art and reflections on art. In an early essay on painting, Artaud declares that works of art "are worth only as much as the conceptions on which they are founded, whose value is exactly what we are calling into question anew." Just as Artaud's work amounts to an *ars poetica* (of which his work is no more than a fragmentary exposition), so he takes art-making to be a trope for the functioning of all consciousness—of life itself.

This trope was the basis of Artaud's affiliation with the Surrealist movement, between 1924 and 1926. As Artaud understood Surrealism, it was a "revolution" applicable to "all states of mind, to all types of human activity," its status as a tendency within the arts being secondary and merely strategic. He welcomed Surrealism—"above all, a state of mind"—as both a critique of mind and a technique for improving the range and quality of the mind. Sensitive as he was in his own life to the repressive workings of the bourgeois idea of day-to-day reality ("We are born, we live, we die in an environment of lies," he wrote in 1923), he was naturally drawn to Surrealism by its advocacy of a more subtle, imaginative, and rebellious consciousness. But he soon found the Surrealist formulas to be another kind of confinement. He got himself expelled when the majority of the Surrealist brotherhood were about to join the French Communist Party—a step that Artaud denounced as a sellout. An actual social revolution changes nothing, he insists scornfully in the polemic he wrote against "the Surrealist bluff" in 1927. The Surrealist adherence to the Third International, though it was to be only of short duration, was a plausible provocation for his quitting the movement, but his dissatisfaction went deeper than a disagreement about what kind of revolution is desirable and relevant. (The Surrealists were hardly more Communist than Artaud was. André Breton had not so much a politics as a set of extremely attractive moral sympathies, which in another period would have brought him to anarchism, and which, quite logically for his own period, led him in the nineteen-thirties to become a partisan and friend of Trotsky.) What really antagonized Artaud was a fundamental difference of temperament.

It was on the basis of a misunderstanding that Artaud had fervently subscribed to the Surrealist challenge to the limits that "reason" sets upon consciousness, and to the Surrealists' faith in the access to a wider consciousness afforded by dreams, drugs, insolent art, and asocial behavior. The Surrealist, he thought, was someone who "despairs of attaining his own mind." He meant himself, of course. Despair is entirely absent from the mainstream of Surrealist attitudes. The Surrealists heralded the benefits that would accrue from unlocking the gates of reason, and ignored the abominations. Artaud, as extravagantly heavy-hearted as the Surrealists were optimistic, could, at most, apprehensively concede legitimacy to the irrational. While the Surrealists proposed exquisite games with consciousness which no one could lose, Artaud was engaged in a mortal struggle to "restore" himself. Breton sanctioned the irrational as a useful route toward a new mental continent. For Artaud, bereft of the hope that he was traveling anywhere, it was the terrain of his martyrdom.

By extending the frontiers of consciousness, the Sur-realists expected not only to refine the rule of reason but to enlarge the yield of physical pleasure. Artaud was incapa-ble of expecting any pleasure from the colonization of new realms of consciousness. In contrast to the Surrealists' euphoric affirmation of both physical passion and romantic love, Artaud regarded eroticism as something threatening, demonic. In *Art and Death* he describes "this preoccupa-tion with sex which petrifies me and rips out my blood." Sexual organs multiply on a monstrous, Brobdingnagian scale and in menacingly hermaphrodite shapes in many of his writings; virginity is treated as a state of grace, and impotence or castration is presented—for example, in the imagery generated by the figure of Abelard in *Art and Death*—as more of a deliverance than a punishment. The Surrealists appeared to love life, Artaud notes haughtily. He felt "contempt" for it. Explaining the program of the Surrealist Research Bureau in 1925, he had favorably de-scribed Surrealism as "a certain order of repulsions," only to conclude the following year that these repulsions were quite shallow. As Marcel Duchamp said in a moving eulogy of his friend Breton in 1966, when Breton died, "the great source of Surrealist inspiration is love: the exal-tation of elective love." Surrealism is a spiritual politics of joy.

Despite Artaud's passionate rejection of Surrealism, his taste was Surrealist—and remained so. His disdain for "realism" as a collection of bourgeois banalities is Sur-realist, and so are his enthusiasms for the art of the mad and the non-professional, for that which comes from the Orient, for whatever is extreme, fantastic, gothic. Artaud's contempt for the dramatic repertory of his time, for the play devoted to exploring the psychology of individual characters—a contempt basic to the argument of the manifestos in *The Theater and Its Double*, written between 1931 and 1936—starts from a position identical with the one from which Breton dismisses the novel in the first "Manifesto of Surrealism" (1924). But Artaud makes a wholly different use of the enthusiasms and the aesthetic prejudices he shares with Breton. The Surrealists are connoisseurs of joy, freedom, pleasure. Artaud is a connoisseur of despair and moral struggle. While the Surrealists explicitly refused to accord art an autonomous value, they perceived no conflict between moral longings and aesthetic ones, and in that sense Artaud is quite right in saying that their program is "aesthetic"—merely aesthetic, he means. Artaud does perceive such a conflict, and demands that art justify itself by the standards of moral seriousness.

From Surrealism, Artaud derives the perspective that links his own perennial psychological crisis with what Breton calls (in the "Second Manifesto of Surrealism," of 1930) "a general crisis of consciousness"—a perspective that Artaud kept throughout his writings. But no sense of crisis in the Surrealist canon is as bleak as Artaud's. Set alongside Artaud's lacerated perceptions, both cosmic and intimately physiological, the Surrealist jeremiads seem tonic rather than alarming. (They are not in fact addressing the same crises. Artaud undoubtedly knew more than Breton about suffering, as Breton knew more than Artaud about freedom.) A related legacy from Surrealism gave Artaud the possibility of continuing throughout his work to take it for granted that art has a "revolutionary" mission. But Artaud's idea of revolution diverges as far from that of the Surrealists as his devastated sensibility does from Breton's essentially wholesome one.

Artaud also retained from the Surrealists the romantic imperative to close the gap between art (and thought) and life. He begins *The Umbilicus of Limbo*, written in 1925, by declaring himself unable to conceive of "work that is detached from life," of "detached creation." But Artaud insists, more aggressively than the Surrealists ever did, on that devaluation of the separate work of art which results from attaching art to life. Like the Surrealists, Artaud regards art as a function of consciousness, each work representing only a fraction of the whole of the artist's consciousness. But by identifying consciousness chiefly with its obscure, hidden, excruciating aspects he makes the dismembering of the totality of consciousness into separate "works" not merely an arbitrary procedure (which is what fascinated the Surrealists) but one that is self-defeating. Artaud's narrowing of the Surrealist view makes a work of art literally useless in itself; insofar as it is considered as a thing, it is dead. In *The Nerve Meter*, also from 1925, Artaud likens his works to lifeless "waste products," mere "scrapings of the soul." These dismembered bits of consciousness acquire value and vitality only as metaphors for works of art; that is, metaphors for consciousness.

Disdaining any detached view of art, any version of that view which regards works of art as objects (to be contemplated, to enchant the senses, to edify, to distract), Artaud assimilates all art to dramatic performance. In Artaud's poetics, art (and thought) is an action—and one that, to be authentic, must be brutal—and also an experience suffered, and charged with extreme emotions. Being both action and passion of this sort, iconoclastic as well as evangelical in its fervor, art seems to require a more daring scene, outside the museums and legitimate showplaces, and a new, ruder form of confrontation with its audience. The rhetoric of inner movement which sustains Artaud's notion of art is impressive, but it does not change the way he actually manages to reject the traditional role of the work of art as an object—by an analysis and an experience of the work of art which are an immense tautology. He sees art as an action, and therefore a passion, of the mind. The mind produces art. And the space in which art is consumed is also the mind—viewed as the organic totality of feeling, physical sensation, and the ability to attribute meaning. Artaud's poetics is a kind of ultimate, manic Hegelianism in which art is the compendium of consciousness, the reflection by consciousness on itself, and the empty space in which consciousness takes its perilous leap of self-transcendence.

Closing the gap between art and life destroys art and, at the same time, universalizes it. In the manifesto that Artaud wrote for the Alfred Jarry Theater, which he founded in 1926, he welcomes "the disrepute into which all forms of art are successively falling." His delight may be a posture, but it would be inconsistent for him to regret that state of affairs. Once the leading criterion for an art becomes its merger with life (that is, everything, including other arts), the existence of separate art forms ceases to be defensible. Furthermore, Artaud assumes that one of the existing arts must soon recover from its failure of nerve and become the total art form, which will absorb all the others. Artaud's lifetime of work may be described as the sequence of his efforts to formulate and inhabit this master art, heroically following out his conviction that the art he sought could hardly be the one—involving language alone—in which his genius was principally confined.

The parameters of Artaud's work in all the arts are identical with the different critical distances he maintains from the idea of an art that is language only—with the diverse forms of his lifelong "revolt against poetry" (the title of a prose text he wrote in Rodez in 1944). Poetry was, chronologically, the first of the many arts he practiced. There are extant poems from as early as 1913, when he was seventeen and still a student in his native Marseilles; his first book, published in 1923, three years after he moved to Paris, was a collection of poems; and it was the unsuccessful submission of some new poems to the *Nouvelle Revue Française* that same year which gave rise to his celebrated correspondence with Rivière. But Artaud soon began slighting poetry in favor of other arts. The dimensions of the poetry he was capable of writing in the twenties were too small for what Artaud intuited to be the scale of a master art. In the early poems, his breath is short; the compact lyric form he employs provides no outlet for his discursive and narrative imagination. Not until the great outburst of writing in the period between 1945 and 1948, in the last three years of his life, did Artaud, by then indifferent to the idea of poetry as a closed lyric statement, find a long-breathed voice that was adequate to the range of his imaginative needs—a voice that was free of established forms and open-ended, like the poetry of Pound. Poetry as Artaud conceived it in the twenties had none of these possibilities or adequacies. It was small, and a total art had to be, to feel, large; it had to be a multi-voiced performance, not a singular lyrical object.

All ventures inspired by the ideal of a total art form— whether in music, painting, sculpture, architecture, or literature—manage in one way to another to theatricalize.

Though Artaud need not have been so literal, it makes sense that at an early age he moved into the explicitly dramatic arts. Between 1922 and 1924, he acted in plays directed by Charles Dullin and the Pitoëffs and in 1924 he also began a career as a film actor. That is to say, by the mid-nineteen-twenties Artaud had two plausible candidates for the role of total art: cinema and theater. However, because it was not as an actor but as a director that he hoped to advance the candidacy of these arts, he soon had to renounce one of them—cinema. Artaud was never given the means to direct a film of his own, and he saw his intentions betrayed in a film of 1928 that was made by another director from one of his screenplays, *The Seashell and the Clergyman*. His sense of defeat was reinforced in 1929 by the arrival of sound, a turning point in the history of film aesthetics which Artaud wrongly prophesied—as did most of the small number of moviegoers who had taken films seriously throughout the nineteen-twenties—would terminate cinema's greatness as an art form. He continued acting in films until 1935, but with little hope of getting a chance to direct his own films and with no further reflection upon the possibilities of cinema (which, regardless of Artaud's discouragement, remains the century's likeliest candidate for the title of master art).

From late 1926 on, Artaud's search for a total art form centered upon the theater. Unlike poetry, an art made out of one material (words), theater uses a plurality of materials: words, light, music, bodies, furniture, clothes. Unlike cinema, an art using only a plurality of languages (images, words, music), theater is carnal, corporeal. Theater brings together the most diverse means—gesture and verbal language, static objects and movement in three-dimensional space. But theater does not become a master art merely by the abundance of its means, however. The prevailing tyranny of some means over others has to be creatively subverted. As Wagner challenged the convention of alternating aria and recitative, which implies a hierarchical relation of speech, song, and orchestral music, Artaud denounced the practice of making every element of the staging serve in some way the words that the actors speak to each other. Assailing as false the priorities of dialogue theater which have subordinated theater to "literature," Artaud implicitly upgrades the means that characterize such other forms of dramatic performance as dance, oratorio, circus, cabaret, church, gymnasium, hospital operating room, courtroom. But annexing these resources from other arts and from quasi-theatrical forms will not make theater a total art form. A master art cannot be constructed by a series of additions; Artaud is not urging mainly that the theater add to its means. Instead, he seeks to purge the theater of what is extraneous or easy. In calling for a theater in which the verbally oriented actor of Europe would be retrained as an "athlete" of the heart, Artaud shows his inveterate taste for spiritual and physical effort—for art as an ordeal.

Artaud's theater is a strenuous machine for transforming the mind's conceptions into entirely "material" events, among which are the passions themselves. Against the centuries-old priority that the European theater has given to words as the means for conveying emotions and ideas, Artaud wants to show the organic basis of emotions and the physicality of ideas—in the bodies of the actors. Artaud's theater is a reaction against the state of underdevelopment in which the bodies (and the voices, apart from talking) of

Western actors have remained for generations, as have the arts of spectacle. To redress the imbalance that so favors verbal language, Artaud proposes to bring the training of actors close to the training of dancers, athletes, mimes, and singers, and "to base the theater on spectacle before everything else," as he says in his "Second Manifesto of the Theater of Cruelty," published in 1933. He is not offering to replace the charms of language with spectacular sets, costumes, music, lighting, and stage effects. Artaud's criterion of spectacle is sensory violence, not sensory enchantment; beauty is a notion he never entertains. Far from considering the spectacular to be in itself desirable, Artaud would commit the stage to an extreme austerity—to the point of excluding anything that stands for something else. "Objects, accessories, sets on the stage must be apprehended directly . . . not for what they represent but for what they are," he writes in a manifesto of 1926. Later, in *The Theater and Its Double*, he suggests eliminating sets altogether. He calls for a "pure" theater, dominated by the "physics of the absolute gesture, which is itself idea."

If Artaud's language sounds vaguely Platonic, it is with good reason, for, like Plato, Artaud approaches art from the moralist's point of view. He does not really like the theater—at least, the theater as it is conceived throughout the West, which he accuses of being insufficiently serious. His theater would have nothing to do with the aim of providing "pointless, artificial diversion," mere entertainment. The contrast at the heart of Artaud's polemics is not between a merely literary theater and a theater of strong sensations but between a hedonistic theater and a theater that is morally rigorous. What Artaud proposes is a theater that Savonarola or Cromwell might well have approved of.

Indeed, *The Theater and Its Double* may be read as an indignant attack on the theater, with an animus reminiscent of the *Letter to d'Alembert* in which Rousseau, enraged by the character of Alceste in *The Misanthrope*— by what he took to be Molière's sophisticated ridiculing of sincerity and moral purity as clumsy fanaticism—ended by arguing that it lay in the nature of theater to be morally superficial. Like Rousseau, Artaud revolted against the moral cheapness of most art. Like Plato, Artaud felt that art generally lies. Artaud will not banish artists from his Republic, but he will countenance art only insofar as it is a "true action." Art must be cognitive. "No image satisfies me unless it is at the same time *knowledge*," he writes. Art must have a beneficial spiritual effect on its audience—an effect whose power depends, in Artaud's view, on a disavowal of all forms of mediation.

It is the moralist in Artaud that makes him urge that the theater be pared down, be kept as free from mediating elements as possible—including the mediation of the written text. Plays tell lies. Even if a play doesn't tell a lie, by achieving the status of a "masterpiece" it *becomes* a lie. Artaud announces in 1926 that he does not want to create a theater to present plays and so perpetuate or add to culture's list of consecrated masterpieces. He judges the heritage of written plays to be a useless obstacle and the playwright an unnecessary intermediary between the audience and the truth that can be presented, naked, on a stage. Here, though, Artaud's moralism takes a distinctly anti-Platonic turn: the naked truth is a truth that is wholly material. Artaud defines the theater as a place where the obscure facets of "the spirit" are revealed in "a real, material projection."

To incarnate thought, a strictly conceived theater must dispense with the mediation of an already written script, thereby ending the separation of author from actor. (This removes the most ancient objection to the actor's profession—that it is a form of psychological debauchery, in which people say words that are not their own and pretend to feel emotions that are functionally insincere.) The separation between actor and audience must be reduced (but not ended), by violating the boundary between the stage area and the auditorium's fixed rows of seats. Artaud, with his hieratic sensibility, never envisages a form of theater in which the audience actively participates in the performance, but he wants to do away with the rules of theatrical decorum which permit the audience to dissociate itself from its own experience. Implicitly answering the moralist's charge that the theater distracts people from their authentic selfhood by leading them to concern themselves with imaginary problems, Artaud wants the theater to address itself neither to the spectators' minds nor to their senses but to their "total existence." Only the most passionate of moralists would have wanted people to attend the theater as they visit the surgeon or the dentist. Though guaranteed not to be fatal (unlike the visit to the surgeon), the operation upon the audience is "serious," and the audience should not leave the theater "intact" morally or emotionally. In another medical image, Artaud compares the theater to the plague. To show the truth means to show archetypes rather than individual psychology; this makes the theater a place of risk, for the "archetypal reality" is "dangerous." Members of the audience are not supposed to identify themselves with what happens on the stage. For Artaud, the "true" theater is a dangerous, intimidating experience—one that excludes placid emotions, playfulness, reassuring intimacy.

The value of emotional violence in art has long been a main tenet of the modernist sensibility. Before Artaud, however, cruelty was exercised mainly in a disinterested spirit, for its aesthetic efficacy. When Baudelaire placed "the shock experience" (to borrow Walter Benjamin's phrase) at the center of his verse and his prose poems, it was hardly to improve or edify his readers. But exactly this was the point of Artaud's devotion to the aesthetics of shock. Through the exclusiveness of his commitment to paroxysmic art, Artaud shows himself to be as much of a moralist about art as Plato—but a moralist whose hopes for art deny just those distinctions in which Plato's view is grounded. As Artaud opposes the separation between art and life, he opposes all theatrical forms that imply a difference between reality and representation. He does not deny the existence of such a difference. But this difference can be vaulted, Artaud implies, if the spectacle is sufficiently—that is, excessively—violent. The "cruelty" of the work of art has not only a directly moral function but a cognitive one. According to Artaud's moralistic criterion for knowledge, an image is true insofar as it is violent.

Plato's view depends on assuming the unbridgeable difference between life and art, reality and representation. In the famous imagery in Book VII of the *Republic*, Plato likens ignorance to living in an ingeniously lit cave, for whose inhabitants life is a spectacle—a spectacle that consists of only the shadows of real events. The cave is a theater. And truth (reality) lies outside it, in the sun. In the Platonic imagery of *The Theater and Its Double*, Artaud takes a more lenient view of shadows and spectacles. He assumes that there are true as well as false shadows (and spectacles), and that one can learn to distinguish between them. Far from identifying wisdom with an emergence from the cave to gaze at a high noon of reality, Artaud thinks that modern consciousness suffers from a lack of shadows. The remedy is to remain in the cave but devise better spectacles. The theater that Artaud proposes will serve consciousness by "naming and directing shadows" and destroying "false shadows" to "prepare the way for a new generation of shadows," around which will assemble "the true spectacle of life."

Not holding a hierarchical view of the mind, Artaud overrides the superficial distinction, cherished by the Surrealists, between the rational and the irrational. Artaud does not speak for the familiar view that praises passion at the expense of reason, the flesh over the mind, the mind exalted by drugs over the prosaic mind, the life of the instincts over deadly cerebration. What he advocates is an alternative relation to the mind. This was the well-advertised attraction that non-Occidental cultures held for Artaud, but it was not what brought him to drugs. (It was to calm the migraines and other neurological pain he suffered from all his life, not to expand his consciousness, that Artaud used opiates, and got addicted.)

For a brief time, Artaud took the Surrealist state of mind as a model for the unified, non-dualistic consciousness he sought. After rejecting Surrealism in 1926, he reproposed art—specifically, theater—as a more rigorous model. The function that Artaud gives the theater is to heal the split between language and flesh. It is the theme of his ideas for training actors: a training antithetical to the familiar one that teaches actors neither how to move nor what to do with their voices apart from talk. (They can scream, growl, sing, chant.) It is also the subject of his ideal dramaturgy. Far from espousing a facile irrationalism that polarizes reason and feeling, Artaud imagines the theater as the place where the body would be reborn in thought and thought would be reborn in the body. He diagnoses his own disease as a split *within* his mind ("My conscious aggregate is broken," he writes) that internalizes the split between mind and body. Artaud's writings on the theater may be read as a psychological manual on the reunification of mind and body. Theater became his supreme metaphor for the self-correcting, spontaneous, carnal, intelligent life of the mind.

Indeed, Artaud's imagery for the theater in *The Theater and Its Double*, written in the nineteen-thirties, echoes images he uses in writings of the early and mid-nineteen-twenties—such as *The Nerve Meter*, letters to René and Yvonne Allendy, and *Fragments of a Diary from Hell*—to describe his own mental pain. Artaud complains that his consciousness is without boundaries and fixed position; bereft of or in a continual struggle with language; fractured—indeed, plagued—by discontinuities; either without physical location or constantly shifting in location (and extension in time and space); sexually obsessed; in a state of violent infestation. Artaud's theater is characterized by an absence of any fixed spatial positioning of the actors vis-à-vis each other and of the actors in relation to the audience; by a fluidity of motion and soul; by the mutilation of language and the transcendence of language in the actor's scream; by the carnality of the spectacle; by its obsessively violent tone. Artaud was, of course, not simply reproducing his inner agony. Rather, he was giving a systematized, positive version of it. Theater is a projected image (necessarily an *ideal* dramatization) of the dangerous, "inhuman" inner life that possessed him, that he struggled so heroically to transcend and to affirm. It is also a homeopathic technique for treating that mangled, passionate inner life. Being a kind of emotional and moral surgery upon consciousness, it must of necessity, according to Artaud, be "cruel."

When Hume expressly likens consciousness to a theater, the image is morally neutral and entirely ahistorical; he is not thinking of any particular kind of theater, Western or other, and would have considered irrelevant any reminder that theater evolves. For Artaud, the decisive part of the analogy is that theater—and consciousness—can change. For not only does consciousness resemble a theater but, as Artaud constructs it, theater resembles consciousness, and therefore lends itself to being turned into a theater-laboratory in which to conduct research in changing consciousness.

Artaud's writings on the theater are transformations of his aspirations for his own mind. He wants theater (like the mind) to be released from confinement "in language and in forms." A liberated theater liberates, he assumes. By giving vent to extreme passions and cultural nightmares, theater exorcises them. But Artaud's theater is by no means simply cathartic. At least in its intention (Artaud's practice in the nineteen-twenties and thirties is another matter), his theater has little in common with the anti-theater of playful, sadistic assault on the audience which was conceived by Marinetti and the Dada artists just before and after World War I. The aggressiveness that Artaud proposes is controlled and intricately orchestrated, for he assumes that sensory violence can be a form of embodied intelligence. By insisting on theater's cognitive function (drama, he writes in 1923, in an essay on Maeterlinck, is "the highest form of mental activity"), he rules out randomness. (Even in his Surrealist days, he did not join in the practice of automatic writing.) Theater, he remarks occasionally, must be "scientific," by which he means that it must not be random, not be merely expressive or spontaneous or personal or entertaining, but must embrace a wholly serious, ultimately religious purpose.

Artaud's insistence on the seriousness of the theatrical situation also marks his difference from the Surrealists, who thought of art and its therapeutic and "revolutionary" mission with a good deal less than precision. The Surrealists, whose moralizing impulses were considerably less intransigent than Artaud's, and who brought no sense of moral urgency at all to bear on art-making, were not moved to search out the limits of any single art form. They tended to be tourists, often of genius, in as many of the arts as possible, believing that the art impulse remains the same wherever it turns up. (Thus, Cocteau, who had the ideal Surrealist career, called everything he did "poetry.") Artaud's greater daring and authority as an aesthetician result partly from the fact that although he, too, practiced several arts, refusing, like the Surrealists, to be inhibited by the distribution of art into different media, he did not regard the various arts as equivalent forms of the same protean impulse. His own activities, however dispersed they may have been, always reflect Artaud's quest for a total art form, into which the others would merge—as art itself would merge into life.

Paradoxically, it was this very denial of independence to

the different territories of art which brought Artaud to do what none of the Surrealists had even attempted: completely rethink one art form. Upon that art, theater, he has had an impact so profound that the course of all recent serious theater in Western Europe and the Americas can be said to divide into two periods—before Artaud and after Artaud. No one who works in the theater now is untouched by the impact of Artaud's specific ideas about the actor's body and voice, the use of music, the role of the written text, the interplay between the space occupied by the spectacle and the audience's space. Artaud changed the understanding of what was serious, what was worth doing. Brecht is the century's only other writer on the theater whose importance and profundity conceivably rival Artaud's. But Artaud did not succeed in affecting the conscience of the modern theater by himself being, as Brecht was, a great director. His influence derives no support from the evidence of his own productions. His practical work in the theater between 1926 and 1935 was apparently so unseductive that it has left virtually no trace, whereas the idea of theater on behalf of which he urged his productions upon an unreceptive public has become ever more potent.

From the mid-nineteen-twenties on, Artaud's work is animated by the idea of a radical change in culture. His imagery implies a medical rather than a historical view of culture: society is ailing. Like Nietzsche, Artaud conceived of himself as a physician to culture—as well as its most painfully ill patient. The theater he planned is a commando action against the established culture, an assault on the bourgeois public; it would both show people that they are dead and wake them up from their stupor. The man who was to be devastated by repeated electric-shock treatments during the last three of nine consecutive years in mental hospitals proposed that theater administer to culture a kind of shock therapy. Artaud, who often complained of feeling paralyzed, wanted theater to renew "the sense of life."

Up to a point, Artaud's prescriptions resemble many programs of cultural renovation that have appeared periodically during the last two centuries of Western culture in the name of simplicity, *élan vital*, naturalness, freedom from artifice. His diagnosis that we live in an inorganic, "petrified culture"—whose lifelessness he associates with the dominance of the written word—was hardly a fresh idea when he stated it; yet, many decades later, it has not exhausted its authority. Artaud's argument in *The Theater and Its Double* is closely related to that of the Nietzsche who in *The Birth of Tragedy* lamented the shriveling of the full-blooded archaic theater of Athens by Socratic philosophy—by the introduction of characters who reason. (Another parallel with Artaud: what made the young Nietzsche an ardent Wagnerian was Wagner's conception of opera as the *Gesamtkunstwerk*—the fullest statement, before Artaud, of the idea of total theater.)

Just as Nietzsche harked back to the Dionysiac ceremonies that preceded the secularized, rationalized, verbal dramaturgy of Athens, Artaud found his models in non-Western religious or magical theater. Artaud does not propose the Theater of Cruelty as a new idea within Western theater. It "assumed . . . another form of civilization." He is referring not to any specific civilization, however, but to an idea of civilization that has numerous bases in history—

a synthesis of elements from past societies and from non-Western and primitive societies of the present. The preference for "another form of civilization" is essentially eclectic. (That is to say, it is a myth generated by certain moral needs.) The inspiration for Artaud's ideas about theater came from Southeast Asia: from seeing the Cambodian theater in Marseilles in 1922 and the Balinese theater in Paris in 1931. But the stimulus could just as well have come from observing the theater of a Dahomey tribe or the shamanistic ceremonies of the Patagonian Indians. What counts is that the other culture be genuinely other; that is, non-Western and non-contemporary.

At different times Artaud followed all three of the most frequently traveled imaginative routes from Western high culture to "another form of civilization." First came what was known just after World War I, in the writings of Hesse, René Daumal, and the Surrealists, as the Turn to the East. Second came the interest in a suppressed part of the Western past—heterodox spiritual or outright magical traditions. Third came the discovery of the life of so-called primitive peoples. What unites the East, the ancient antinomian and occult traditions in the West, and the exotic communitarianism of pre-literate tribes is that they are elsewhere, not only in space but in time. All three embody the values of the past. Though the Tarahumara Indians in Mexico still exist, their survival in 1936, when Artaud visited them, was already anachronistic; the values that the Tarahumara represent belong as much to the past as do those of the ancient Near Eastern mystery religions that Artaud studied while writing his historical novel *Heliogabalus*, in 1933. The three versions of "another form of civilization" bear witness to the same search for a society integrated around overtly religious themes, and flight from the secular. What interests Artaud is the Orient of Buddhism (see his "Letter to the Buddhist Schools," written in 1925) and of Yoga; it would never be the Orient of Mao Tse-tung, however much Artaud talked up revolution. (The Long March was taking place at the very time that Artaud was struggling to mount the productions of his Theater of Cruelty in Paris.)

This nostalgia for a past often so eclectic as to be quite unlocatable historically is a facet of the modernist sensibility which has seemed increasingly suspect in recent decades. It is an ultimate refinement of the colonialist outlook: an imaginative exploitation of non-white cultures, whose moral life it drastically oversimplifies, whose wisdom it plunders and parodies. To that criticism there is no convincing reply. But to the criticism that the quest for "another form of civilization" refuses to submit to the disillusionment of accurate historical knowledge, one can make an answer. It never sought such knowledge. The other civilizations are being used as models and are available as stimulants to the imagination precisely because they are *not* accessible. They are both models and mysteries. Nor can this quest be dismissed as fraudulent on the ground that it is insensitive to the political forces that cause human suffering. It consciously opposes such sensitivity. This nostalgia forms part of a view that is deliberately *not* political—however frequently it brandishes the word "revolution."

One result of the aspiration to a total art which follows from denying the gap between art and life has been to encourage the notion of art as an instrument of revolution. The other result has been the identification of both art and life with disinterested, pure playfulness. For every Vertov or Breton, there is a Cage or a Duchamp or a Rauschenberg. Although Artaud is close to Vertov and Breton in that he considers his activities to be part of a larger revolution, as a self-proclaimed revolutionary in the arts he actually stands between two camps—not interested in satisfying either the political or the ludic impulse. Dismayed when Breton attempted to link the Surrealist program with Marxism, Artaud broke with the Surrealists for what he considered to be their betrayal, into the hands of politics, of an essentially "spiritual" revolution. He was anti-bourgeois almost by reflex (like nearly all artists in the modernist tradition), but the prospect of transferring power from the bourgeoisie to the proletariat never tempted him. From his avowedly "absolute" viewpoint, a change in social structure would not change anything. The revolution to which Artaud subscribes has nothing to do with politics but is conceived explicitly as an effort to redirect culture. Not only does Artaud share the widespread (and mistaken) belief in the possibility of a cultural revolution unconnected with political change but he implies that the *only* genuine cultural revolution is one having nothing to do with politics.

Artaud's call to cultural revolution suggests a program of heroic regression similar to that formulated by every great *anti*-political moralist of our time. The banner of cultural revolution is hardly a monopoly of the Marxist or Maoist left. On the contrary, it appeals particularly to apolitical thinkers and artists (like Nietzsche, Spengler, Pirandello, Marinetti, D. H. Lawrence, Pound) who more commonly become right-wing enthusiasts. On the political left, there are few advocates of cultural revolution. (Tatlin, Gramsci, and Godard are among those who come to

mind.) A radicalism that is purely "cultural" is either il-
lusory or, finally, conservative in its implications. Artaud's
plans for subverting and revitalizing culture, his longing
for a new type of human personality illustrate the limits of
all thinking about revolution which is anti-political.

Cultural revolution that refuses to be political has nowhere to go but toward a theology of culture—and a
soteriology. "I aspire to another life," Artaud declares in
1927. All Artaud's work is about salvation, theater being
the means of saving souls which he meditated upon most
deeply. Spiritual transformation is a goal on whose behalf
theater has often been enlisted in this century, at least
since Isadora Duncan. In the most recent and solemn example, the Laboratory Theater of Jerzy Grotowski, the
whole activity of building a company and rehearsing and
putting on plays serves the spiritual reeducation of the
actors; the presence of an audience is required only to witness the feats of self-transcendence that the actors perform.
In Artaud's Theater of Cruelty, it is the audience that will
be twice-born—an untested claim, since Artaud never made
his theater work (as Grotowski did throughout the nineteen-
sixties in Poland). As a goal, it seems a good deal less
feasible than the discipline for which Grotowski aims. Sensitive as Artaud is to the emotional and physical armoring of
the conventionally trained actor, he never examines closely
how the radical retraining he proposes will affect the actor
as a human being. His thought is all for the audience.

As might have been expected, the audience proved to be
a disappointment. Artaud's productions in the two theaters
he founded, the Alfred Jarry Theater and the Theater of
Cruelty, created little involvement. Yet, although entirely
dissatisfied with the quality of his public, Artaud com-

plained much more about the token support he got from the serious Paris theater establishment (he had a long, desperate correspondence with Louis Jouvet), about the difficulty of getting his projects produced at all, about the paltriness of their success when they were put on. Artaud was understandably embittered because, despite a number of titled patrons, and friends who were eminent writers, painters, editors, directors—all of whom he constantly badgered for moral support and money—his work, when it was actually produced, enjoyed only a small portion of the acclaim conventionally reserved for properly sponsored, difficult events attended by the regulars of high-culture consumption. Artaud's most ambitious, fully articulated production of the Theater of Cruelty, his own *The Cenci*, lasted for seventeen days in the spring of 1935. But had it run for a year he would probably have been equally convinced that he had failed.

In modern culture, powerful machinery has been set up whereby dissident work, after gaining an initial semi-official status as "avant-garde," is gradually absorbed and rendered acceptable. But Artaud's practical activities in the theater barely qualified for this kind of cooptation. *The Cenci* is not a very good play, even by the standards of convulsive dramaturgy which Artaud sponsored, and the interest of his production of *The Cenci*, by all accounts, lay in ideas it suggested but did not actually embody. What Artaud did on the stage as a director and as a leading actor in his productions was too idiosyncratic, narrow, and hysterical to persuade. He has exerted influence through his ideas about the theater, a constituent part of the authority of these ideas being precisely his inability to put them into practice.

Fortified by its insatiable appetite for novel commodities, the educated public of great cities has become habituated to the modernist agony and well skilled in outwitting it: any negative can eventually be turned into a positive. Thus Artaud, who urged that the repertory of masterpieces be thrown on the junk pile, has been extremely influential as the creator of an alternative repertory, an adversary tradition of plays. Artaud's stern cry "No more masterpieces!" has been heard as the more conciliatory "No more of *those* masterpieces!" But this positive recasting of his attack on the traditional repertory has not taken place without help from Artaud's practice (as distinct from his rhetoric). Despite his repeated insistence that the theater should dispense with plays, his own work in the theater was far from playless. He named his first company after the author of *King Ubu*. Apart from his own projects—*The Conquest of Mexico* and *The Capture of Jerusalem* (unproduced) and *The Cenci*—there were a number of then unfashionable or obscure masterpieces that Artaud wanted to revive. He did get to stage the two great "dream plays" by Calderón and Strindberg (*Life Is a Dream* and *A Dream Play*), and over the years he hoped also to direct productions of Euripides (*The Bacchae*), Seneca (*Thyestes*), *Arden of Feversham*, Shakespeare (*Macbeth, Richard II, Titus Andronicus*), Tourneur (*The Revenger's Tragedy*), Webster (*The White Devil, The Duchess of Malfi*), Sade (an adaptation of *Eugénie de Franval*), Büchner (*Woyzeck*), and Hölderlin (*The Death of Empedocles*). This selection of plays delineates a now familiar sensibility. Along with the Dadaists, Artaud formulated the taste that was eventually to become standard serious taste—Off-Broadway, Off-Off-Broadway, in university theaters. In terms of the past, it meant dethroning Sophocles and Corneille and Racine in favor of Euripides and the dark Elizabethans; the only dead French writer on Artaud's list is Sade. In the last fifteen years, that taste has been represented in the Happenings and the Theater of the Ridiculous; the plays of Genet, Jean Vauthier, Arrabal, Carmelo Bene, and Sam Shepard; and such celebrated productions as the Living Theater's *Frankenstein*, Eduardo Manet's *The Nuns* (directed by Roger Blin), Michael McClure's *The Beard*, Robert Wilson's *Deafman Glance*, and Heathcote Williams's *ac/dc*. Whatever Artaud did to subvert the theater, and to segregate his own work from other, merely aesthetic currents in the interests of establishing its spiritual hegemony, could still be assimilated as a new theatrical tradition, and mostly has been.

If Artaud's project does not actually transcend art, it presupposes a goal that art can sustain only temporarily. Each use of art in a secular society for the purposes of spiritual transformation, insofar as it is made *public*, is inevitably robbed of its true adversary power. Stated in directly, or even indirectly, religious language, the project is notably vulnerable. But atheist projects for spiritual transformation, such as the political art of Brecht, have proved to be equally cooptable. Only a few situations in modern secular society seem sufficiently extreme and uncommunicative to have a chance of evading cooptation. Madness is one. Suffering that surpasses the imaginable (like the Holocaust) is another. A third is, of course, silence. One way to stop this inexorable process of ingestion is to break off communication (even anti-communication). An exhaustion of the impulse to use art as a medium of spiritual transformation is almost inevitable—as in the temptation felt by every modern author when confronted with the indifference or mediocrity of the public, on the one hand, or the ease of success, on the other, to stop writing altogether. Thus, it was not just for lack of money or support within the profession that, after putting on *The Cenci*, in 1935, Artaud abandoned the theater. The project of creating in a secular culture an institution that can manifest a dark, hidden reality is a contradiction in terms. Artaud was never able to found his Bayreuth—though he would have liked to—for his ideas are the kind that cannot be institutionalized.

The year after the failure of *The Cenci*, Artaud embarked on a trip to Mexico to witness that demonic reality in a still existing "primitive" culture. Unsuccessful at embodying this reality in a spectacle to impose on others, he became a spectator of it himself. From 1935 onward, Artaud lost touch with the promise of an ideal art form. His writings, always didactic, now took on a prophetic tone and referred frequently to esoteric magical systems, like the Cabala and tarot. Apparently, Artaud came to believe that he could exercise directly, in his own person, the emotional power (and achieve the spiritual efficacy) he had wanted for the theater. In the middle of 1937, he traveled to the Aran Islands, with an obscure plan for exploring or confirming his magic powers. The wall between art and life was still down. But instead of everything being assimilated into art, the movement swung the other way; and Artaud moved without mediation into his life—a dangerous, careering object, the vessel of a raging hunger for total transformation which could never find its appropriate nourishment.

Nietzsche coolly assumed an atheist theology of the spirit, a negative theology, a mysticism without God. Artaud wandered in the labyrinth of a specific type of religious sensibility, the Gnostic one. (Central to Mithraism, Manichaeism, Zoroastrianism, and Tantric Buddhism, but pushed to the heretical margins of Judaism, Christianity, and Islam, the perennial Gnostic thematics appear in the different religions in different terminologies but with certain common lines.) The leading energies of Gnosticism come from metaphysical anxiety and acute psychological distress—the sense of being abandoned, of being an alien, of being possessed by demonic powers which prey on the human spirit in a cosmos vacated by the divine. The cosmos is itself a battlefield, and each human life exhibits the conflict between the repressive, persecuting forces from without and the feverish, afflicted individual spirit seeking redemption. The demonic forces of the cosmos exist as physical matter. They also exist as "law," taboos, prohibitions. Thus, in the Gnostic metaphors the spirit is abandoned, fallen, trapped in a body, and the individual is repressed, trapped by being in "the world"—what we would call "society." (It is a mark of all Gnostic thinking to polarize inner space, the psyche, and a vague outer space, "the world" or "society," which is identified with repression—making little or no acknowledgment of the importance of the mediating levels of the various social spheres and institutions.) The self, or spirit, discovers itself in the break with "the world." The only freedom possible is an inhuman, desperate freedom. To be saved, the spirit must be taken out of its body, out of its personality, out of "the world." And freedom requires an arduous preparation. Whoever seeks it must both accept extreme humiliation and exhibit the greatest spiritual pride. In one version, freedom entails total asceticism. In another ver-

sion, it entails libertinism—practicing the art of transgres-
sion. To be free of "the world," one must break the moral
(or social) law. To transcend the body, one must pass
through a period of physical debauchery and verbal blasphemy, on the principle that only when morality has been
deliberately flouted is the individual capable of a radical
transformation: entering into a state of grace that leaves all
moral categories behind. In both versions of the exemplary
Gnostic drama, someone who is saved is beyond good and
evil. Founded on an exacerbation of dualisms (body-mind,
matter-spirit, evil-good, dark-light), Gnosticism promises
the abolition of all dualisms.

Artaud's thought reproduces most of the Gnostic
themes. For example, his attack on Surrealism in the polemic written in 1927 is couched in a language of cosmic
drama, in which he refers to the necessity of a "displace-
ment of the spiritual center of the world" and to the origin
of all matter in "a spiritual deviation." Throughout his
writings, Artaud speaks of being persecuted, invaded, and
defiled by alien powers; his work focuses on the vicissitudes
of the spirit as it constantly discovers its lack of liberty in
its very condition of being "matter." Artaud is obsessed
with physical matter. From *The Nerve Meter* and *Art and
Death*, written in the nineteen-twenties, to *Here Lies* and
the radio play *To Have Done with the Judgment of God*,
written in 1947–48, Artaud's prose and poetry depict a
world clogged with matter (shit, blood, sperm), a defiled
world. The demonic powers that rule the world are incarnated in matter, and matter is "dark." Essential to the
theater that Artaud conceives—a theater devoted to myth
and magic—is his belief that all the great myths are "dark"
and that all magic is black magic. Even when life is en-

crusted by petrified, degenerate, merely verbal language, Artaud insists, the reality lies just underneath—or somewhere else. Art can tap these powers, for they seethe in every psyche. It was in search of these dark powers that Artaud went to Mexico in 1936 to witness the Tarahumara peyote rites. The individual's salvation requires making contact with the malevolent powers, submitting to them, and suffering at their hands in order to triumph over them.

What Artaud admires in the Balinese theater, he writes in 1931, is that it has nothing to do with "entertainment" but, rather, has "something of the ceremonial quality of a religious rite." Artaud is one of many directors in this century who have sought to re-create theater as ritual, to give theatrical performances the solemnity of religious transactions, but usually one finds only the vaguest, most promiscuous idea of religion and rite, which imputes to a Catholic mass and a Hopi rain dance the same artistic value. Artaud's vision, while perhaps not any more feasible in modern secular society than the others, is at least more specific as to the kind of rite involved. The theater Artaud wants to create enacts a secularized Gnostic rite. It is not an expiation. It is not a sacrifice, or, if it is, the sacrifices are all metaphors. It is a rite of transformation—the communal performance of a violent act of spiritual alchemy. Artaud summons the theater to renounce "psychological man, with his well-dissected character and feelings, and social man, submissive to laws and misshapen by religions and precepts," and to address itself only "to total man"—a thoroughly Gnostic notion.

Whatever Artaud's wishes for "culture," his thinking ultimately shuts out all but the private self. Like the Gnostics, he is a radical individualist. From his earliest writings, his concern is with a metamorphosis of the "inner" state of the soul. (The self is, by definition, an "inner self.") Mundane relations, he assumes, do not touch the kernel of the individual; the search for redemption undercuts all social solutions.

The one instrument of redemption of a possibly social character which Artaud considers is art. The reason he is not interested in a humanistic theater, a theater about individuals, is that he believes that such a theater can never effect any radical transformation. To be spiritually liberating, Artaud thinks, theater has to express impulses that are larger than life. But this only shows that Artaud's idea of freedom is itself a Gnostic one. Theater serves an "inhuman" individuality, an "inhuman" freedom, as Artaud calls it in *The Theater and Its Double*—the very opposite of the liberal, sociable idea of freedom. (That Artaud found Breton's thinking shallow—that is, optimistic, aesthetic—follows from the fact that Breton did not have a Gnostic style or sensibility. Breton was attracted by the hope of reconciling the demands of individual freedom with the need to expand and balance the personality through generous, corporate emotions; the anarchist view, formulated in this century with the greatest subtlety and authority by Breton and Paul Goodman, is a form of conservative, humanistic thinking—doggedly sensitive to everything repressive and mean while remaining loyal to the limits that protect human growth and pleasure. The mark of Gnostic thinking is that it is enraged by *all* limits, even those that save.) "All true freedom is dark," Artaud says in *The Theater and Its Double*, "and is infallibly identified with sexual freedom, which is also dark, although we do not know precisely why."

Both the obstacle to and the locus of freedom, for Artaud, lie in the body. His attitude covers the familiar Gnostic thematic range: the affirmation of the body, the revulsion from the body, the wish to transcend the body, the quest for the redeemed body. "Nothing touches me, nothing interests me," he writes, "except what addresses itself *directly* to my flesh." But the body is always a problem. Artaud never defines the body in terms of its capacity for sensuous pleasure but always in terms of its electric capacity for intelligence and for pain. As Artaud laments, in *Art and Death*, that his mind is ignorant of his body, that he lacks ideas that conform to his "condition as a physical animal," so he complains that his body is ignorant of his mind. In Artaud's imagery of distress, body and spirit prevent each other from being intelligent. He speaks of the "intellectual cries" that come from his flesh, source of the only knowledge he trusts. Body has a mind. "There is a mind in the flesh," he writes, "a mind quick as lightning."

It is what Artaud expects intellectually from the body that leads to his recoil from the body—the ignorant body. Indeed, each attitude implies the other. Many of the poems express a profound revulsion from the body, and accumulate loathsome evocations of sex. "A true man has no sex," Artaud writes in a text published in December 1947. "He ignores this hideousness, this stupefying sin." *Art and Death* is perhaps the most sex-obsessed of all his works, but Artaud demonized sexuality in everything he wrote. The most common presence is a monstrous, obscene body— "this unusable body made out of meat and crazy sperm," he calls it in *Here Lies*. Against this fallen body, defiled by matter, he sets the fantasied attainment of a pure body— divested of organs and vertiginous lusts. Even while insisting that he is nothing but his body, Artaud expresses a fervent longing to transcend it altogether, to abandon his sexuality. In other imagery, the body must be made intelligent, respiritualized. Recoiling from the defiled body, he appeals to the redeemed body in which thought and flesh will be unified: "It is through the skin that metaphysics will be made to reenter our minds"; only the flesh can supply "a definitive understanding of Life." The Gnostic task of the theater that Artaud imagines is nothing less than to create this redeemed body—a mythic project that he explains by referring to that last great Gnostic systematics, Renaissance alchemy. As the alchemists, obsessed with the problem of matter in classically Gnostic terms, sought methods of changing one kind of matter into another (higher, spiritualized) kind of matter, so Artaud sought to create an alchemical arena that operates on the flesh as much as on the spirit. Theater is the exercise of a "terrible and dangerous act," he says in "Theater and Science"—"THE REAL ORGANIC AND PHYSICAL TRANSFORMATION OF THE HUMAN BODY."

Artaud's principal metaphors are classically Gnostic. Body is mind turned into "matter." As the body weighs down and deforms the soul, so does language, for language is thought turned into "matter." The problem of language, as Artaud poses it to himself, is identical with the problem of matter. The disgust for the body and the revulsion against words are two forms of the same feeling. In the equivalences established by Artaud's imagery, sexuality is the corrupt, fallen activity of the body, and "literature" is the corrupt, fallen activity of words. Although Artaud never entirely stopped hoping to use activities in the arts as a means of spiritual liberation, art was always suspect—

like the body. And Artaud's hope for art is also Gnostic, like his hope for the body. The vision of a total art has the same form as the vision of the redemption of the body. ("The body is the body/it is alone/it has no need of organs," Artaud writes in one of his last poems.) Art will be redemptive when, like the redeemed body, it transcends itself—when it has no organs (genres), no different parts. In the redeemed art that Artaud imagines, there are no separate works of art—only a total art environment, which is magical, paroxysmic, purgative, and, finally, opaque.

Gnosticism, a sensibility organized around the idea of knowing (gnosis) rather than around faith, sharply distinguishes between exoteric and esoteric knowledge. The adept must pass through various levels of instruction to be worthy of being initiated into the true doctrine. Knowledge, which is identified with the capacity for self-transformation, is reserved for the few. It is natural that Artaud, with his Gnostic sensibility, should have been attracted to numerous secret doctrines, as both an alternative to and a model for art. During the nineteen-thirties, Artaud, an amateur polymath of great energy, read more and more about esoteric systems—alchemy, tarot, the Cabala, astrology, Rosicrucianism. What these doctrines have in common is that they are all relatively late, decadent transformations of the Gnostic thematics. From Renaissance alchemy Artaud drew a model for his theater: like the symbols of alchemy, theater describes "philosophical states of matter" and attempts to transform them. Tarot, to give another example, supplied the basis of *The New Revelations of Being*, written in 1937, just before his seven-week trip to Ireland; it was the last work he wrote before the mental breakdown that resulted in his confinement when he was returned to France. But none of these already formulated, schematic, historically fossilized secret doctrines could contain the convulsions of the living Gnostic imagination in Artaud's head.

Only the exhausting is truly interesting. Artaud's basic ideas are crude; what gives them their power is the intricacy and eloquence of his self-analysis, unequaled in the history of the Gnostic imagination. And, for the first time, the Gnostic themes can be seen in evolution. Artaud's work is particularly precious as the first complete documentation of someone *living through* the trajectory of Gnostic thought. The result, of course, is a terrible smash.

The last refuge (historically, psychologically) of Gnostic thought is in the constructions of schizophrenia. With Artaud's return from Ireland to France began nine years of imprisonment in mental hospitals. Evidence, mainly from letters he wrote to his two principal psychiatrists at Rodez, Dr. Gaston Ferdière and Dr. Jacques Latrémolière, shows how literally his thought followed the Gnostic formulas. In the ecstatic fantasies of this period, the world is a maelstrom of magical substances and forces; his consciousness becomes a theater of screaming struggle between angels and demons, virgins and whores. His horror of the body now unmodulated, Artaud explicitly identifies salvation with virginity, sin with sex. As Artaud's elaborate religious speculations during the Rodez period may be read as metaphors for paranoia, so paranoia may be read as a metaphor for an exacerbated religious sensibility of the Gnostic type. The literature of the crazy in this century is a rich religious literature—perhaps the last original zone of genuine Gnostic speculation.

When Artaud was let out of the asylum, in 1946, he still

considered himself the victim of a conspiracy of demonic powers, the object of an extravagant act of persecution by "society." Although the wave of schizophrenia had receded to the point of no longer swamping him, his basic metaphors were still intact. In the two years of life that remained to him, Artaud forced them to their logical conclusion.

In 1944, still in Rodez, Artaud had recapitulated his Gnostic complaint against language in a short text, "Revolt Against Poetry." Returning to Paris in 1946, he longed to work again in the theater, to recover the vocabulary of gesture and spectacle; but in the short time left to him he had to resign himself to speaking with language only. Artaud's writings of this last period—virtually unclassifiable as to genre: there are "letters" that are "poems" that are "essays" that are "dramatic monologues"—give the impression of a man attempting to step out of his own skin. Passages of clear, if hectic, argument alternate with passages in which words are treated primarily as material (sound): they have a magical value. (Attention to the sound and shape of words, as distinct from their meaning, is an element of the Cabalistic teaching of the *Zohar*, which Artaud had studied in the nineteen-thirties.) Artaud's commitment to the magical value of words explains his refusal of metaphor as the principal mode of conveying meaning in his late poems. He demands that language directly express the physical human being. The person of the poet appears in a state beyond nakedness: flayed.

As Artaud reaches toward the unspeakable, his imagination coarsens. Yet his last works, in their mounting obsession with the body and their ever more explicit loathing of sex, still stand in a direct line with the early writings, in which there is, parallel to the mentalization of the body, a corresponding sexualization of consciousness. What Artaud wrote between 1946 and 1948 only extends metaphors he used throughout the nineteen-twenties—of mind as a body that never allows itself to be "possessed," and of the body as a kind of demonic, writhing, brilliant mind. In Artaud's fierce battle to transcend the body, everything is eventually turned into the body. In his fierce battle to transcend language, everything is eventually turned into language. Artaud, describing the life of the Tarahumara Indians, translates nature itself into a language. In the last writings, the obscene identity of the flesh and the word reaches an extremity of loathing—notably in the play commissioned by French radio, *To Have Done with the Judgment of God*, which was then banned on the eve of its projected broadcast in February 1948. (Artaud was still revising it a month later, when he died.) Talking, talking, talking, Artaud expresses the most ardent revulsion against talk—and the body.

The Gnostic passage through the stages of transcendence implies a move from the conventionally intelligible to what is conventionally unintelligible. Gnostic thinking characteristically reaches for an ecstatic speech that dispenses with distinguishable words. (It was the adoption by the Christian church in Corinth of a Gnostic form of preaching—"speaking in tongues"—that provoked Paul's remonstrations in the First Epistle to the Corinthians.) The language Artaud used at the end of his life, in passages in *Artaud le Mômo*, *Here Lies*, and *To Have Done with the Judgment of God*, verges on an incandescent declamatory speech beyond sense. "All true language is incomprehensible," Artaud says in *Here Lies*. He is not seeking a universal language, as Joyce did. Joyce's view of language was historical, ironic, whereas Artaud's view is medical, tragic. The unintelligible in *Finnegans Wake* not only is decipherable, with effort, but is meant to be deciphered. The unintelligible parts of Artaud's late writings are supposed to remain obscure—to be directly apprehended as sound.

The Gnostic project is a search for wisdom, but a wisdom that cancels itself out in unintelligibility, loquacity, and silence. As Artaud's life suggests, all schemes for ending dualism, for a unified consciousness at the Gnostic level of intensity, are eventually bound to fail—that is, their practitioners collapse into what society calls madness or into silence or suicide. (Another example: the vision of a totally unified consciousness expressed in the gnomic messages Nietzsche sent to friends in the weeks before his complete mental collapse in Turin in 1889.) The project transcends the limits of the mind. Thus, while Artaud still desperately reaffirms his effort to unify his flesh and his mind, the terms of his thinking imply the annihilation of consciousness. In the writings of this last period, the cries from his fractured consciousness and his martyred body reach a pitch of inhuman intensity and rage.

Artaud offers the greatest *quantity* of suffering in the history of literature. So drastic and pitiable are the numerous descriptions he gives of his pain that readers, overwhelmed, may be tempted to distance themselves by remembering that Artaud was crazy.

In whatever sense he ended up being mad, Artaud had been mad all his life. He had a history of internment in mental hospitals from mid-adolescence on—well before he arrived in Paris from Marseilles, in 1920, at the age of twenty-four, to begin his career in the arts; his lifelong addiction to opiates, which may have aggravated his mental disorder, had probably begun before this date. Lacking the saving knowledge that allows most people to be conscious with relatively little pain—the knowledge of what Rivière calls "the blessed opacity of experience" and "the innocence of facts"—Artaud at no time in his life wholly got out from under the lash of madness. But simply to judge Artaud mad—reinstating the reductive psychiatric wisdom —means to reject Artaud's argument.

Psychiatry draws a clear line between art (a "normal" psychological phenomenon, manifesting objective aesthetic limits) and symptomatology: the very boundary that Artaud contests. Writing to Rivière in 1923, Artaud insists on raising the question of the autonomy of his art—of whether, despite his avowed mental deterioration, despite that "fundamental flaw" in his own psyche which sets him apart from other people, his poems do nevertheless exist *as poems*, not just as psychological documents. Rivière replies by expressing confidence that Artaud, despite his mental distress, will one day become a good poet. Artaud answers impatiently, changing his ground: he wants to close the gap between life and art implicit in his original question and in Rivière's well-intentioned but obtuse encouragement. He decides to defend his poems as they are—for the merit they possess just because they don't quite make it as art.

The task of the reader of Artaud is not to react with the distance of Rivière—as if madness and sanity could communicate with each other only on sanity's own ground, in the language of reason. The values of sanity are not eternal or "natural," any more than there is a self-evident, common-sense meaning to the condition of being insane. The perception that some people are crazy is part of the history of thought, and madness requires a historical definition. Madness means not making sense—means saying what doesn't have to be taken seriously. But this depends entirely on how a given culture defines sense and seriousness; the definitions have varied widely through history. What is called insane denotes that which in the determination of a particular society must not be thought. Madness is a concept that fixes limits; the frontiers of madness define what is "other." A mad person is someone whose voice society doesn't want to listen to, whose behavior is intolerable, who ought to be suppressed. Different societies use different definitions of what constitutes madness (that is, of what does not make sense). But no definition is less provincial than any other. Part of the outrage over the current practice in the Soviet Union of locking up political dissenters in insane asylums is misplaced, in that it holds not only that doing so is wicked (which is true) but that doing so is a fraudulent use of the concept of mental illness; it is assumed that there is a universal, correct, scientific standard of sanity (the one enforced in the mental-health policies of, say, the United States, England, and Sweden, rather than the one enforced in those of a country like Morocco). This is simply not true. In every society, the definitions of sanity and madness are arbitrary—are, in the largest sense, political.

Artaud was extremely sensitive to the repressive function of the concept of madness. He saw the insane as the heroes and martyrs of thought, stranded at the vantage point of extreme social (rather than merely psychological) alienation, volunteering for madness—as those who, through a superior conception of honor, prefer to go mad rather than forfeit a certain lucidity, an extreme passionateness in presenting their convictions. In a letter to Jacqueline Breton from the hospital in Ville-Evrard in April 1939, after a year and a half of what was to be nine years of confinement, he wrote, "I am a fanatic, I am not a madman." But any fanaticism that is not a group fanaticism is precisely what society understands as madness.

Madness is the logical conclusion of the commitment to individuality when that commitment is pushed far enough. As Artaud puts it in the "Letter to the Medical Directors of Lunatic Asylums" in 1925, "all individual acts are antisocial." It is an unpalatable truth, perhaps quite irreconcilable with the humanist ideology of capitalist democracy or of social democracy or of liberal socialism—but Artaud is right. Whenever behavior becomes sufficiently individual, it will become objectively anti-social and will seem, to other people, mad. All human societies agree on this point. They differ only on how the standard of madness is applied, and on who are protected or partly exempted (for reasons of economic, social, sexual, or cultural privilege) from the penalty of imprisonment meted out to those whose basic anti-social act consists in not making sense.

The insane person has a dual identity in Artaud's works: the ultimate victim, and the bearer of a subversive wisdom. In his preface, written in 1946, to the proposed Gallimard collected edition of his writings, he describes himself as one of the mentally underprivileged, grouping lunatics with aphasiacs and illiterates. Elsewhere in the writings of his last two years, he repeatedly situates himself in the company of the mentally hyper-endowed who have gone mad —Hölderlin, Nerval, Nietzsche, and van Gogh. Insofar as

the genius is simply an extension, and intensification, of
the individual, Artaud suggests the existence of a natural
affinity between genius and madness in a far more precise
sense than the romantics did. But while denouncing the
society that imprisons the mad, and affirming madness as
the outward sign of a profound spiritual exile, he never
suggests that there is anything liberating in losing one's
mind.

Some of his writings, particularly the early Surrealist
texts, take a more positive attitude toward madness. In
"General Security: The Liquidation of Opium," for instance, he seems to be defending the practice of a deliber-
ate derangement of the mind and senses (as Rimbaud once
defined the poet's vocation). But he never stops saying—in
the letters to Rivière, to Dr. Allendy, and to George Soulié
de Morant in the nineteen-twenties and nineteen-thirties,
in the letters written between 1943 and 1945 from Rodez,
and in the essay on van Gogh written in 1947, some months
after his release from Rodez—that madness is confining,
destroying. Mad people may know the truth—so much
truth that society takes its revenge on these unhappy seers
by outlawing them. But being mad is also unending pain, a
state to be transcended—and it is that pain which Artaud
renders, imposing it on his readers.

To read Artaud through is nothing less than an ordeal.
Understandably, readers seek to protect themselves with
reductions and applications of his work. It demands a special stamina, a special sensitivity, and a special tact to read
Artaud properly. It is not a question of giving one's assent
to Artaud—this would be shallow—or even of neutrally
"understanding" him and his relevance. What is there to
assent to? How could anyone assent to Artaud's ideas un-

less one was already in the demonic state of siege that he was in? Those ideas were emitted under the intolerable pressure of his own situation. Not only is Artaud's position not tenable; it is not a "position" at all.

Artaud's thought is organically part of his singular, haunted, impotent, savagely intelligent consciousness. Artaud is one of the great, daring mapmakers of consciousness *in extremis*. To read him properly does not require believing that the *only* truth that art can supply is one that is singular and is authenticated by extreme suffering. Of art that describes other states of consciousness—less idiosyncratic, less exalted, perhaps no less profound—it is correct to ask that it yield general truths. But the exceptional cases at the limit of "writing"—Sade is one, Artaud is another—demand a different approach. What Artaud has left behind is work that cancels itself, thought that outbids thought, recommendations that cannot be enacted. Where does that leave the reader? Still with a body of work, even though the character of Artaud's writings forbids their being treated simply as "literature." Still with a body of thought, even though Artaud's thought forbids assent—as his aggressively self-immolating personality forbids identification. Artaud shocks, and, unlike the Surrealists, he remains shocking. (Far from being subversive, the spirit of the Surrealists is ultimately constructive and falls well within the humanist tradition, and their stagy violations of bourgeois proprieties were not dangerous, truly asocial acts. Compare the behavior of Artaud, who really was impossible socially.) To detach his thought as a portable intellectual commodity is just what that thought explicitly prohibits. It is an event, rather than an object.

Forbidden assent or identification or appropriation or

imitation, the reader can only fall back on the category of inspiration. "INSPIRATION CERTAINLY EXISTS," as Artaud affirms in capital letters in *The Nerve Meter*. One can be inspired by Artaud. One can be scorched, changed by Artaud. But there is no way of applying Artaud.

Even in the domain of the theater, where Artaud's presence can be decanted into a program and a theory, the work of those directors who have most benefited from his ideas shows there is no way to use Artaud that stays true to him. Not even Artaud himself found the way; by all accounts, his own stage productions were far from being up to the level of his ideas. And for the many people not connected with the theater—mainly the anarchist-minded, for whom Artaud has been especially important—the experience of his work remains profoundly private. Artaud is someone who has made a spiritual trip for us—a shaman. It would be presumptuous to reduce the geography of Artaud's trip to what can be colonized. Its authority lies in the parts that yield nothing for the reader except intense discomfort of the imagination.

Artaud's work becomes usable according to our needs, but the work vanishes behind our use of it. When we tire of using Artaud, we can return to his writings. "Inspiration in stages," he says. "One mustn't let in too much literature."

All art that expresses a radical discontent and aims at shattering complacencies of feeling risks being disarmed, neutralized, drained of its power to disturb—by being admired, by being (or seeming to be) too well understood, by becoming relevant. Most of the once exotic themes of Artaud's work have within the last decade become loudly topical: the wisdom (or lack of it) to be found in drugs,

Oriental religions, magic, the life of North American Indians, body language, the insanity trip; the revolt against "literature," and the belligerent prestige of non-verbal arts; the appreciation of schizophrenia; the use of art as violence against the audience; the necessity for obscenity. Artaud in the nineteen-twenties had just about every taste (except enthusiasms for comic books, science fiction, and Marxism) that was to become prominent in the American counterculture of the nineteen-sixties, and what he was reading in that decade—the *Tibetan Book of the Dead*, books on mysticism, psychiatry, anthropology, tarot, astrology, Yoga, acupuncture—is like a prophetic anthology of the literature that has recently surfaced as popular reading among the advanced young. But the current relevance of Artaud may be as misleading as the obscurity in which his work lay until now.

Unknown outside a small circle of admirers ten years ago, Artaud is a classic today. He is an example of a willed classic—an author whom the culture attempts to assimilate but who remains profoundly indigestible. One use of literary respectability in our time—and an important part of the complex career of literary modernism—is to make acceptable an outrageous, essentially forbidding author, who becomes a classic on the basis of the many interesting things to be said about the work that scarcely convey (perhaps even conceal) the real nature of the work itself, which may be, among other things, extremely boring or morally monstrous or terribly painful to read. Certain authors become literary or intellectual classics because they are *not* read, being in some intrinsic way unreadable. Sade, Artaud, and Wilhelm Reich belong in this company: authors who were jailed or locked up in insane asylums because they were screaming, because they were out of control; immoderate, obsessed, strident authors who repeat themselves endlessly, who are rewarding to quote and read bits of, but who overpower and exhaust if read in large quantities.

Like Sade and Reich, Artaud is relevant and understandable, a cultural monument, as long as one mainly refers to his ideas without reading much of his work. For anyone who reads Artaud through, he remains fiercely out of reach, an unassimilable voice and presence.

(1973)

Fascinating Fascism

I

First Exhibit. Here is a book of 126 splendid color photographs by Leni Riefenstahl, certainly the most ravishing book of photographs published anywhere in recent years. In the intractable mountains of the southern Sudan live about eight thousand aloof, godlike Nuba, emblems of physical perfection, with large, well-shaped, partly shaven heads, expressive faces, and muscular bodies that are depilated and decorated with scars; smeared with sacred gray-white ash, the men prance, squat, brood, wrestle on the arid slopes. And here is a fascinating layout of twelve black-and-white photographs of Riefenstahl on the back cover of *The Last of the Nuba*, also ravishing, a chronological sequence of expressions (from sultry inwardness to the grin of a Texas matron on safari) vanquishing the intractable march of aging. The first photograph was taken in 1927 when she was twenty-five and already a movie star, the most recent are dated 1969 (she is cuddling a naked African baby) and 1972 (she is holding a camera), and each of them shows some version of an ideal presence, a kind of imperishable beauty, like Elisabeth Schwarzkopf's, that only gets gayer and more metallic and healthier-looking with old age. And here is a biographical sketch of Riefenstahl on the dust jacket, and an introduction (unsigned) entitled "How Leni Riefenstahl came to study the Mesakin Nuba of Kordofan"—full of disquieting lies.

The introduction, which gives a detailed account of Riefenstahl's pilgrimage to the Sudan (inspired, we are told, by reading Hemingway's *The Green Hills of Africa* "one sleepless night in the mid-1950s"), laconically identifies the photographer as "something of a mythical figure as a film-maker before the war, half-forgotten by a nation which chose to wipe from its memory an era of its history." Who (one hopes) but Riefenstahl herself could have thought up this fable about what is mistily referred to as "a nation" which for some unnamed reason "chose" to perform the deplorable act of cowardice of forgetting "an era"—tactfully left unspecified—"of its history"? Presumably, at least some readers will be startled by this coy allusion to Germany and the Third Reich.

Compared with the introduction, the jacket of the book is positively expansive on the subject of the photographer's career, parroting misinformation that Riefenstahl has been dispensing for the last twenty years.

It was during Germany's blighted and momentous 1930s that Leni Riefenstahl sprang to international fame as a film director. She was born in 1902, and her first devotion was to creative dancing. This led to her participation in silent films, and soon she was herself making—and starring in—her own talkies, such as *The Mountain* (1929).

These tensely romantic productions were widely admired, not least by Adolf Hitler who, having attained power in 1933, commissioned Riefenstahl to make a documentary on the Nuremberg Rally in 1934.

It takes a certain originality to describe the Nazi era as "Germany's blighted and momentous 1930s," to summarize the events of 1933 as Hitler's "having attained power," and to assert that Riefenstahl, most of whose work was in its own decade correctly identified as Nazi propaganda, enjoyed "international fame as a film director," ostensibly like her contemporaries Renoir, Lubitsch, and Flaherty. (Could the publishers have let LR write the jacket copy herself? One hesitates to entertain so unkind a thought, although "her first devotion was to creative dancing" is a phrase few native speakers of English would be capable of.)

The facts are, of course, inaccurate or invented. Not only did Riefenstahl not make—or star in—a talkie called *The Mountain* (1929). No such film exists. More generally: Riefenstahl did not first simply participate in silent films and then, when sound came in, begin directing and starring in her own films. In all nine films she ever acted in, Riefenstahl was the star; and seven of these she did not direct. These seven films were: *The Holy Mountain* (*Der heilige Berg*, 1926), *The Big Jump* (*Der grosse Sprung*,

1927), *The Fate of the House of Habsburg* (*Das Schicksal derer von Habsburg*, 1929), *The White Hell of Pitz Palü* (*Die weisse Hölle von Piz Palü*, 1929)—all silents— followed by *Avalanche* (*Stürme über dem Montblanc*, 1930), *White Frenzy* (*Der weisse Rausch*, 1931), and *S.O.S. Iceberg* (*S.O.S. Eisberg*, 1932–1933). All but one were directed by Arnold Fanck, *auteur* of hugely successful Alpine epics since 1919, who made only two more films, both flops, after Riefenstahl left him to strike out on her own as a director in 1932. (The film not directed by Fanck is *The Fate of the House of Habsburg*, a royalist weepie made in Austria in which Riefenstahl played Marie Vetsera, Crown Prince Rudolf's companion at Mayerling. No print seems to have survived.)

Fanck's pop-Wagnerian vehicles for Riefenstahl were not just "tensely romantic." No doubt thought of as apolitical when they were made, these films now seem in retrospect, as Siegfried Kracauer has pointed out, to be an anthology of proto-Nazi sentiments. Mountain climbing in Fanck's films was a visually irresistible metaphor for unlimited aspiration toward the high mystic goal, both beautiful and terrifying, which was later to become concrete in Führer-worship. The character that Riefenstahl generally played was that of a wild girl who dares to scale the peak that others, the "valley pigs," shrink from. In her first role, in the silent *The Holy Mountain* (1926), that of a young dancer named Diotima, she is wooed by an ardent climber who converts her to the healthy ecstasies of Alpinism. This character underwent a steady aggrandizement. In her first sound film, *Avalanche* (1930), Riefenstahl is a mountain-possessed girl in love with a young meteorologist, whom she rescues when a storm strands him in his observatory on Mont Blanc.

Riefenstahl herself directed six films, the first of which, *The Blue Light* (*Das blaue Licht*, 1932), was another mountain film. Starring in it as well, Riefenstahl played a role similar to the ones in Fanck's films for which she had been so "widely admired, not least by Adolf Hitler," but allegorizing the dark themes of longing, purity, and death that Fanck had treated rather scoutishly. As usual, the mountain is represented as both supremely beautiful and dangerous, that majestic force which invites the ultimate affirmation of and escape from the self—into the brotherhood of courage and into death. The role Riefenstahl devised for herself is that of a primitive creature who has a unique relation to a destructive power: only Junta, the rag-clad outcast girl of the village, is able to reach the mysterious blue light radiating from the peak of Mount Cristallo, while other young villagers, lured by the light, try to climb the mountain and fall to their deaths. What eventually causes the girl's death is not the impossibility of the goal symbolized by the mountain but the materialist, prosaic spirit of envious villagers and the blind rationalism of her lover, a well-meaning visitor from the city.

The next film Riefenstahl directed after *The Blue Light* was not "a documentary on the Nuremberg Rally in 1934" —Riefenstahl made four non-fiction films, not two, as she has claimed since the 1950s and as most current whitewashing accounts of her repeat—but *Victory of the Faith* (*Sieg des Glaubens*, 1933), celebrating the first National Socialist Party Congress held after Hitler seized power. Then came the first of two works which did indeed make her internationally famous, the film on the next National Socialist Party Congress, *Triumph of the Will* (*Triumph des Willens*, 1935)—whose title is never mentioned on the jacket of *The Last of the Nuba*—after which she made a short film (eighteen minutes) for the army, *Day of Freedom: Our Army* (*Tag der Freiheit: Unsere Wehrmacht*, 1935), that depicts the beauty of soldiers and soldiering for the Führer. (It is not surprising to find no mention of this film, a print of which was found in 1971; during the 1950s and 1960s, when Riefenstahl and everyone else believed *Day of Freedom* to have been lost, she had it dropped from her filmography and refused to discuss it with interviewers.)

The jacket copy continues:

> Riefenstahl's refusal to submit to Goebbels' attempt to subject her visualisation to his strictly propagandistic requirements led to a battle of wills which came to a head when Riefenstahl made her film of the 1936 Olympic Games, Olympia. This, Goebbels attempted to destroy; and it was only saved by the personal intervention of Hitler.
>
> With two of the most remarkable documentaries of the 1930s to her credit, Riefenstahl continued making films of her devising, unconnected with the rise of Nazi Germany, until 1941, when war conditions made it impossible to continue.
>
> Her acquaintance with the Nazi leadership led to her arrest at the end of the Second World War: she was tried twice, and acquitted twice. Her reputation was in eclipse, and she was half forgotten—although to a whole generation of Germans her name had been a household word.

Except for the bit about her having once been a household word in Nazi Germany, not one part of the above is true.

To cast Riefenstahl in the role of the individualist-artist, defying philistine bureaucrats and censorship by the patron state ("Goebbels' attempt to subject her visualisation to his strictly propagandistic requirements") should seem like nonsense to anyone who has seen *Triumph of the Will*—a film whose very conception negates the possibility of the filmmaker's having an aesthetic conception independent of propaganda. The facts, denied by Riefenstahl since the war, are that she made *Triumph of the Will* with unlimited facilities and unstinting official cooperation (there was never any struggle between the filmmaker and the German minister of propaganda). Indeed, Riefenstahl was, as she relates in the short book about the making of *Triumph of the Will*, in on the planning of the rally—which was from the start conceived as the set of a film spectacle.* *Olympia*—a three-and-a-half-hour film in two parts, *Festival of the People (Fest der Völker)* and *Festival of Beauty (Fest der Schönheit)*—was no less an official production. Riefenstahl has maintained in interviews since the 1950s that *Olympia* was commissioned by the International

---

* Leni Riefenstahl, *Hinter den Kulissen des Reichparteitag-Films* (Munich, 1935). A photograph on page 31 shows Hitler and Riefenstahl bending over some plans, with the caption: "The preparations for the Party Congress were made hand in hand with the preparations for the camera work." The rally was held on September 4–10; Riefenstahl relates that she began work in May, planning the film sequence by sequence, and supervising the construction of elaborate bridges, towers, and tracks for the cameras. In late August, Hitler came to Nuremberg with Viktor Lutze, head of the SA, "for an inspection and to give final instructions." Her thirty-two cameramen were dressed in SA uniforms throughout the shooting, "a suggestion of the Chief of Staff [Lutze], so that no one will disturb the solemnity of the image with his civilian clothing." The SS supplied a team of guards.

Olympic Committee, produced by her own company, and made over Goebbels's protests. The truth is that *Olympia* was commissioned and entirely financed by the Nazi government (a dummy company was set up in Riefenstahl's name because it was thought unwise for the government to appear as the producer) and facilitated by Goebbels's ministry at every stage of the shooting*; even the plausible-sounding legend of Goebbels objecting to her footage of the triumphs of the black American track star Jesse Owens is untrue. Riefenstahl worked for eighteen months on the editing, finishing in time so that the film could have its world premiere on April 29, 1938, in Berlin, as part of the festivities for Hitler's forty-ninth birthday; later that year *Olympia* was the principal German entry at the Venice Film Festival, where it won the Gold Medal.

More lies: to say that Riefenstahl "continued making films of her devising, unconnected with the rise of Nazi Germany, until 1941." In 1939 (after returning from a visit to Hollywood, the guest of Walt Disney), she accompanied the invading Wehrmacht into Poland as a uniformed army war correspondent with her own camera team; but there is no record of any of this material surviving the war. After *Olympia* Riefenstahl made exactly one more film, *Tiefland* (*Lowland*), which she began in 1941 —and, after an interruption, resumed in 1944 (in the Barrandov Film Studios in Nazi-occupied Prague), and finished in 1954. Like *The Blue Light*, *Tiefland* opposes lowland or valley corruption to mountain purity, and once

---

* See Hans Barkhausen, "Footnote to the History of Riefenstahl's 'Olympia,'" *Film Quarterly*, Fall 1974—a rare act of informed dissent amid the large number of tributes to Riefenstahl that have appeared in American and Western European film magazines during the last few years.

again the protagonist (played by Riefenstahl) is a beautiful outcast. Riefenstahl prefers to give the impression that there were only two documentaries in a long career as a director of fiction films, but the truth is that four of the six films she directed were documentaries made for and financed by the Nazi government.

It is hardly accurate to describe Riefenstahl's professional relationship to and intimacy with Hitler and Goebbels as "her acquaintance with the Nazi leadership." Riefenstahl was a close friend and companion of Hitler's well before 1932; she was a friend of Goebbels, too: no evidence supports Riefenstahl's persistent claim since the 1950s that Goebbels hated her, or even that he had the power to interfere with her work. Because of her unlimited personal access to Hitler, Riefenstahl was precisely the only German filmmaker who was not responsible to the Film Office (Reichsfilmkammer) of Goebbels's ministry of propaganda. Last, it is misleading to say that Riefenstahl was "tried twice, and acquitted twice" after the war. What happened is that she was briefly arrested by the Allies in 1945 and two of her houses (in Berlin and Munich) were seized. Examinations and court appearances started in 1948, continuing intermittently until 1952, when she was finally "de-Nazified" with the verdict: "No political activity in support of the Nazi regime which would warrant punishment." More important: whether or not Riefenstahl deserved a prison sentence, it was not her "acquaintance" with the Nazi leadership but her activities as a leading propagandist for the Third Reich that were at issue.

The jacket copy of *The Last of the Nuba* summarizes faithfully the main line of the self-vindication which Riefenstahl fabricated in the 1950s and which is most fully spelled out in the interview she gave to *Cahiers du Cinéma* in September 1965. There she denied that any of her work was propaganda—calling it cinema verité. "Not a single scene is staged," Riefenstahl says of *Triumph of the Will*. "Everything is genuine. And there is no tendentious commentary for the simple reason that there is no commentary at all. It is *history—pure history*." We are a long way from that vehement disdain for "the chronicle-film," mere "reportage" or "filmed facts," as being unworthy of the event's "heroic style" which is expressed in her book on the making of the film.*

---

* If another source is wanted—since Riefenstahl now claims (in an interview in the German magazine *Filmkritik*, August 1972) that she didn't write a single word of *Hinter den Kulissen des Reichparteitag-Films*, or even read it at the time—there is an interview in the *Völkischer Beobachter*, August 26, 1933, about her filming of the 1933 Nuremberg rally, where she makes similar declarations.

Riefenstahl and her apologists always talk about *Triumph of the Will* as if it were an independent "documentary," often citing technical problems encountered while filming to prove she had enemies among the party leadership (Goebbels's hatred), as if such difficulties were not a normal part of filmmaking. One of the more dutiful reruns of the myth of Riefenstahl as mere documentarist— and political innocent—is the *Filmguide to "Triumph of the Will"* published in the Indiana University Press Filmguide Series, whose author, Richard Meram Barsam, concludes his preface by expressing his "gratitude to Leni Riefenstahl herself, who cooperated in many hours of interviews, opened her archive to my research, and took a genuine interest in this book." Well might she take an interest in a book whose opening chapter is "Leni Riefenstahl and the Burden of Independence," and whose theme is "Riefenstahl's belief that the artist must, at all costs, remain independent of the material world. In her own life, she has achieved artistic freedom, but at a great cost." Etc.

As an antidote, let me quote an unimpeachable source (at least he's not here to say he didn't write it)—Adolf Hitler. In his brief preface to *Hinter den Kulissen*, Hitler describes *Triumph of the Will* as "a totally unique and incomparable glorification of the power and beauty of our Movement." And it is.

Although *Triumph of the Will* has no narrative voice, it does open with a written text heralding the rally as the redemptive culmination of German history. But this opening statement is the least original of the ways in which the film is tendentious. It has no commentary because it doesn't need one, for *Triumph of the Will* represents an already achieved and radical transformation of reality: history become theater. How the 1934 Party convention was staged was partly determined by the decision to produce *Triumph of the Will*—the historic event serving as the set of a film which was then to assume the character of an authentic documentary. Indeed, when some of the footage of Party leaders at the speakers' rostrum was spoiled, Hitler gave orders for the shots to be refilmed; and Streicher, Rosenberg, Hess, and Frank histrionically repledged their fealty to the Führer weeks later, without Hitler and without an audience, on a studio set built by Speer. (It is altogether correct that Speer, who built the gigantic site of the rally on the outskirts of Nuremberg, is listed in the credits of *Triumph of the Will* as architect of the film.) Anyone who defends Riefenstahl's films as documentaries, if documentary is to be distinguished from propaganda, is being ingenuous. In *Triumph of the Will*, the document (the image) not only is the record of reality but is one reason for which the reality has been constructed, and must eventually supersede it.

The rehabilitation of proscribed figures in liberal societies does not happen with the sweeping bureaucratic finality of the *Soviet Encyclopedia*, each new edition of which brings forward some hitherto unmentionable figures and lowers an equal or greater number through the trap door of nonexistence. Our rehabilitations are smoother, more insinuative. It is not that Riefenstahl's Nazi past has suddenly become acceptable. It is simply that, with the turn of the cultural wheel, it no longer matters. Instead of dispensing a freeze-dried version of history from above, a liberal society settles such questions by waiting for cycles of taste to distill out the controversy.

The purification of Leni Riefenstahl's reputation of its Nazi dross has been gathering momentum for some time, but it has reached some kind of climax this year, with Riefenstahl the guest of honor at a new cinéphile-controlled film festival held in the summer in Colorado and the subject of a stream of respectful articles and interviews in newspapers and on TV, and now with the publication of *The Last of the Nuba*. Part of the impetus behind Riefenstahl's recent promotion to the status of a cultural monument surely owes to the fact that she is a woman. The 1973 New York Film Festival poster, made by a well-known artist who is also a feminist, showed a blond doll-woman whose right breast is encircled by three names: Agnès Leni Shirley. (That is, Varda, Riefenstahl, Clarke.) Feminists would feel a pang at having to sacrifice the one woman who made films that everybody acknowledges to be first-rate. But the strongest impetus behind the change in attitude toward Riefenstahl lies in the new, ampler fortunes of the idea of the beautiful.

The line taken by Riefenstahl's defenders, who now include the most influential voices in the avant-garde film establishment, is that she was always concerned with beauty. This, of course, has been Riefenstahl's own contention for some years. Thus the *Cahiers du Cinéma* interviewer set Riefenstahl up by observing fatuously that what *Triumph of the Will* and *Olympia* "have in common is that they both give form to a certain reality, itself based on a certain idea of form. Do you see anything peculiarly German about this concern for form?" To this, Riefenstahl answered:

> I can simply say that I feel spontaneously attracted by everything that is beautiful. Yes: beauty, harmony. And perhaps this care for composition, this aspiration to form is in effect something very German. But I don't know these things myself, exactly. It comes from the unconscious and not from my knowledge. . . . What do you want me to add? Whatever is purely realistic, slice-of-life, which is average, quotidian, doesn't interest me. . . . I am fascinated by what is beautiful, strong, healthy, what is living. I seek harmony. When harmony is produced I am happy. I believe, with this, that I have answered you.

That is why *The Last of the Nuba* is the last, necessary step in Riefenstahl's rehabilitation. It is the final rewrite of the past; or, for her partisans, the definitive confirmation that she was always a beauty freak rather than a horrid propagandist.* Inside the beautifully produced book, photo-

---

* This is how Jonas Mekas (*The Village Voice*, October 31, 1974) salutes the publication of *The Last of the Nuba*: "Riefenstahl continues her celebration—or is it a search?—of the classical beauty of the human body, the search which she began in her films. She is interested in the ideal, in the monumental." Mekas in the same paper on November 7, 1974: "And here is my own final statement on Riefenstahl's films: If you are an idealist, you'll see idealism in her films; if you are a classicist, you'll see in her films an ode to classicism; if you are a Nazi, you'll see in her films Nazism."

graphs of the perfect, noble tribe. And on the jacket, photographs of "my perfect German woman" (as Hitler called Riefenstahl), vanquishing the slights of history, all smiles.

Admittedly, if the book were not signed by Riefenstahl one would not necessarily suspect that these photographs had been taken by the most interesting, talented, and effective artist of the Nazi era. Most people who leaf through *The Last of the Nuba* will probably see it as one more lament for vanishing primitives—the greatest example remains Lévi-Strauss in *Tristes Tropiques* on the Bororo Indians in Brazil—but if the photographs are examined carefully, in conjunction with the lengthy text written by Riefenstahl, it becomes clear that they are continuous with her Nazi work. Riefenstahl's particular slant is revealed by her choice of this tribe and not another: a people she describes as acutely artistic (everyone owns a lyre) and beautiful (Nuba men, Riefenstahl notes, "have an athletic build rare in any other African tribe"); endowed as they are with "a much stronger sense of spiritual and religious relations than of worldly and material matters," their principal activity, she insists, is ceremonial. *The Last of the Nuba* is about a primitivist ideal: a portrait of a people subsisting in a pure harmony with their environment, untouched by "civilization."

All four of Riefenstahl's commissioned Nazi films—whether about Party congresses, the Wehrmacht, or athletes—celebrate the rebirth of the body and of community, mediated through the worship of an irresistible leader. They follow directly from the films of Fanck in which she starred and her own *The Blue Light.* The Alpine fictions are tales of longing for high places, of the challenge and ordeal of the elemental, the primitive; they are about the vertigo before power, symbolized by the majesty and beauty of mountains. The Nazi films are epics of achieved community, in which everyday reality is transcended through ecstatic self-control and submission; they are about the triumph of power. And *The Last of the Nuba*, an elegy for the soon-to-be extinguished beauty and mystic powers of primitives whom Riefenstahl calls "her adopted people," is the third in her triptych of fascist visuals.

In the first panel, the mountain films, heavily dressed people strain upward to prove themselves in the purity of the cold; vitality is identified with physical ordeal. For the middle panel, the films made for the Nazi government: *Triumph of the Will* uses overpopulated wide shots of massed figures alternating with close-ups that isolate a single passion, a single perfect submission: in a temperate zone clean-cut people in uniforms group and regroup, as if they were seeking the perfect choreography to express their fealty. In *Olympia*, the richest visually of all her films (it uses both the verticals of the mountain films and the horizontal movements characteristic of *Triumph of the Will*), one straining, scantily clad figure after another seeks the ecstasy of victory, cheered on by ranks of compatriots in the stands, all under the still gaze of the benign Super-Spectator, Hitler, whose presence in the stadium consecrates this effort. (*Olympia*, which could as well have been called *Triumph of the Will*, emphasizes that there are no easy victories.) In the third panel, *The Last of the Nuba*, the almost naked primitives, awaiting the final ordeal of their proud heroic community, their imminent extinction, frolic and pose under the scorching sun.

It is Götterdämmerung time. The central events in

Nuba society are wrestling matches and funerals: vivid encounters of beautiful male bodies and death. The Nuba, as Riefenstahl interprets them, are a tribe of aesthetes. Like the henna-daubed Masai and the so-called Mudmen of New Guinea, the Nuba paint themselves for all important social and religious occasions, smearing on a white-gray ash which unmistakably suggests death. Riefenstahl claims to have arrived "just in time," for in the few years since these photographs were taken the glorious Nuba have been corrupted by money, jobs, clothes. (And, probably, by war—which Riefenstahl never mentions, since what she cares about is myth not history. The civil war that has been tearing up that part of the Sudan for a dozen years must have scattered new technology and a lot of detritus.)

Although the Nuba are black, not Aryan, Riefenstahl's portrait of them evokes some of the larger themes of Nazi ideology: the contrast between the clean and the impure, the incorruptible and the defiled, the physical and the mental, the joyful and the critical. A principal accusation against the Jews within Nazi Germany was that they were urban, intellectual, bearers of a destructive corrupting "critical spirit." The book bonfire of May 1933 was launched with Goebbels's cry: "The age of extreme Jewish intellectualism has now ended, and the success of the German revolution has again given the right of way to the German spirit." And when Goebbels officially forbade art criticism in November 1936, it was for having "typically Jewish traits of character": putting the head over the heart, the individual over the community, intellect over feeling. In the transformed thematics of latter-day fascism, the Jews no longer play the role of defiler. It is "civilization" itself.

What is distinctive about the fascist version of the old
idea of the Noble Savage is its contempt for all that is reflective, critical, and pluralistic. In Riefenstahl's casebook
of primitive virtue, it is hardly—as in Lévi-Strauss—the
intricacy and subtlety of primitive myth, social organiza-
tion, or thinking that is being extolled. Riefenstahl
strongly recalls fascist rhetoric when she celebrates the
ways the Nuba are exalted and unified by the physical or-
deals of their wrestling matches, in which the "heaving and
straining" Nuba men, "huge muscles bulging," throw one
another to the ground—fighting not for material prizes but
"for the renewal of the sacred vitality of the tribe."
Wrestling and the rituals that go with it, in Riefenstahl's
account, bind the Nuba together. Wrestling

> is the expression of all that distinguishes the Nuba
> way of life. . . . Wrestling generates the most pas-
> sionate loyalty and emotional participation in the
> team's supporters, who are, in fact, the entire "non-
> playing" population of the village. . . . Its impor-
> tance as the expression of the total outlook of the
> Mesakin and Korongo cannot be exaggerated; it is
> the expression in the visible and social world of the
> invisible world of the mind and of the spirit.

In celebrating a society where the exhibition of physical
skill and courage and the victory of the stronger man over
the weaker are, as she sees it, the unifying symbols of the
communal culture—where success in fighting is the "main
aspiration of a man's life"—Riefenstahl seems hardly to
have modified the ideas of her Nazi films. And her portrait
of the Nuba goes further than her films in evoking one as-

pect of the fascist ideal: a society in which women are merely breeders and helpers, excluded from all ceremonial functions, and represent a threat to the integrity and strength of men. From the "spiritual" Nuba point of view (by the Nuba Riefenstahl means, of course, males), contact with women is profane; but, ideal society that this is supposed to be, the women know their place.

> The fiancées or wives of the wrestlers are as concerned as the men to avoid any intimate contact . . . their pride at being the bride or wife of a strong wrestler supersedes their amorousness.

Lastly, Riefenstahl is right on target with her choice as a photographic subject of a people who "look upon death as simply a matter of fate—which they do not resist or struggle against," of a society whose most enthusiastic and lavish ceremonial is the funeral. Viva la muerte.

It may seem ungrateful and rancorous to refuse to cut loose *The Last of the Nuba* from Riefenstahl's past, but there are salutary lessons to be learned from the continuity of her work as well as from that curious and implacable recent event—her rehabilitation. The careers of other artists who became fascists, such as Céline and Benn and Marinetti and Pound (not to mention those, like Pabst and Pirandello and Hamsun, who embraced fascism in the decline of their powers), are not instructive in a comparable way. For Riefenstahl is the only major artist who was completely identified with the Nazi era and whose work, not only during the Third Reich but thirty years after its fall, has consistently illustrated many themes of fascist aesthetics.

Fascist aesthetics include but go far beyond the rather special celebration of the primitive to be found in *The Last of the Nuba*. More generally, they flow from (and justify) a preoccupation with situations of control, submissive behavior, extravagant effort, and the endurance of pain; they endorse two seemingly opposite states, egomania and servitude. The relations of domination and enslavement take the form of a characteristic pageantry: the massing of groups of people; the turning of people into things; the multiplication or replication of things; and the grouping of people/things around an all-powerful, hypnotic leader-figure or force. The fascist dramaturgy centers on the orgiastic transactions between mighty forces and their puppets, uniformly garbed and shown in ever swelling numbers. Its choreography alternates between ceaseless motion and a congealed, static, "virile" posing. Fascist art glorifies surrender, it exalts mindlessness, it glamorizes death.

Such art is hardly confined to works labeled as fascist or produced under fascist governments. (To cite films only: Walt Disney's *Fantasia*, Busby Berkeley's *The Gang's All Here*, and Kubrick's *2001* also strikingly exemplify certain formal structures and themes of fascist art.) And, of course, features of fascist art proliferate in the official art of communist countries—which always presents itself under the banner of realism, while fascist art scorns realism in the name of "idealism." The tastes for the monumental and for mass obeisance to the hero are common to both fascist and communist art, reflecting the view of all totalitarian regimes that art has the function of "immortalizing" its leaders and doctrines. The rendering of movement in grandiose and rigid patterns is another element in common, for such choreography rehearses the very unity of the polity. The masses are made to take form, be design. Hence mass athletic demonstrations, a choreographed display of bodies, are a valued activity in all totalitarian countries; and the art of the gymnast, so popular now in Eastern Europe, also evokes recurrent features of fascist aesthetics; the holding in or confining of force; military precision.

In both fascist and communist politics, the will is staged publicly, in the drama of the leader and the chorus. What is interesting about the relation between politics and art under National Socialism is not that art was subordinated to political needs, for this is true of dictatorships both of the right and of the left, but that politics appropriated the rhetoric of art—art in its late romantic phase. (Politics is "the highest and most comprehensive art there is," Goebbels said in 1933, "and we who shape modern German policy feel ourselves to be artists . . . the task of art and the artist [being] to form, to give shape, to remove the diseased and create freedom for the healthy.") What is interesting about art under National Socialism are those features which make it a special variant of totalitarian art. The official art of countries like the Soviet Union and China aims to expound and reinforce a utopian morality. Fascist art displays a utopian aesthetics—that of physical perfection. Painters and sculptors under the Nazis often depicted the nude, but they were forbidden to show any bodily imperfections. Their nudes look like pictures in physique magazines: pinups which are both sanctimoniously asexual and (in a technical sense) pornographic, for they have the perfection of a fantasy. Riefenstahl's promotion of the beautiful and the healthy, it must be said, is much more sophisticated than this; and never witless, as it is in other Nazi visual art. She appreciates a range of bodily types—in matters of beauty she is not racist—and in *Olympia* she does show some effort and strain, with its attendant imperfections, as well as stylized, seemingly effortless exertions (such as diving, in the most admired sequence of the film).

In contrast to the asexual chasteness of official communist art, Nazi art is both prurient and idealizing. A utopian aesthetics (physical perfection; identity as a biological given) implies an ideal eroticism: sexuality converted into the magnetism of leaders and the joy of followers. The fascist ideal is to transform sexual energy into a "spiritual" force, for the benefit of the community. The erotic (that is, women) is always present as a temptation, with the most admirable response being a heroic repression of the sexual impulse. Thus Riefenstahl explains why Nuba marriages, in contrast to their splendid funerals, involve no ceremonies or feasts.

> A Nuba man's greatest desire is not union with a woman but to be a good wrestler, thereby affirming the principle of abstemiousness. The Nuba dance ceremonies are not sensual occasions but rather "festivals of chastity"—of containment of the life force.

Fascist aesthetics is based on the containment of vital forces; movements are confined, held tight, held in.

Nazi art is reactionary, defiantly outside the century's mainstream of achievement in the arts. But just for this reason it has been gaining a place in contemporary taste. The left-wing organizers of a current exhibition of Nazi painting and sculpture (the first since the war) in Frankfurt have found, to their dismay, the attendance excessively large and hardly as serious-minded as they had hoped. Even when flanked by didactic admonitions from Brecht and by concentration-camp photographs, what Nazi art reminds these crowds of is—other art of the 1930s, notably Art Deco. (Art Nouveau could never be a fascist style; it is, rather, the prototype of that art which fascism defines as decadent; the fascist style at its best is Art Deco, with its sharp lines and blunt massing of material, its petrified eroticism.) The same aesthetic responsible for the bronze colossi of Arno Breker—Hitler's (and, briefly, Cocteau's) favorite sculptor—and of Josef Thorak also produced the muscle-bound Atlas in front of Manhattan's Rockefeller Center and the faintly lewd monument to the fallen doughboys of World War I in Philadelphia's Thirtieth Street railroad station.

To an unsophisticated public in Germany, the appeal of Nazi art may have been that it was simple, figurative, emotional; not intellectual; a relief from the demanding complexities of modernist art. To a more sophisticated public, the appeal is partly to that avidity which is now bent on retrieving all the styles of the past, especially the most pilloried. But a revival of Nazi art, following the revivals of Art Nouveau, Pre-Raphaelite painting, and Art Deco, is most unlikely. The painting and sculpture are not just sententious; they are astonishingly meager as art. But precisely these qualities invite people to look at Nazi art with knowing and sniggering detachment, as a form of Pop Art.

Riefenstahl's work is free of the amateurism and naïveté one finds in other art produced in the Nazi era, but it still promotes many of the same values. And the same very

modern sensibility can appreciate her as well. The ironies
of pop sophistication make for a way of looking at
Riefenstahl's work in which not only its formal beauty but
its political fervor are viewed as a form of aesthetic excess.
And alongside this detached appreciation of Riefenstahl is
a response, whether conscious or unconscious, to the
subject itself, which gives her work its power.

Triumph of the Will and *Olympia* are undoubtedly
superb films (they may be the two greatest documentaries
ever made), but they are not really important in the history
of cinema as an art form. Nobody making films today
alludes to Riefenstahl, while many filmmakers (including
myself) regard Dziga Vertov as an inexhaustible provocation and source of ideas about film language. Yet it is
arguable that Vertov—the most important figure in documentary films—never made a film as purely effective and
thrilling as *Triumph of the Will* or *Olympia*. (Of course,
Vertov never had the means at his disposal that Riefenstahl had. The Soviet government's budget for propaganda
films in the 1920s and early 1930s was less than lavish.)

In dealing with propagandistic art on the left and on the
right, a double standard prevails. Few people would admit
that the manipulation of emotion in Vertov's later films and
in Riefenstahl's provides similar kinds of exhilaration.
When explaining why they are moved, most people are
sentimental in the case of Vertov and dishonest in the case
of Riefenstahl. Thus Vertov's work evokes a good deal of
moral sympathy on the part of his cinéphile audiences all
over the world; people consent to be moved. With Riefenstahl's work, the trick is to filter out the noxious political
ideology of her films, leaving only their "aesthetic" merits.
Praise of Vertov's films always presupposes the knowledge

that he was an attractive person and an intelligent and original artist-thinker, eventually crushed by the dictatorship which he served. And most of the contemporary audience for Vertov (as for Eisenstein and Pudovkin) assumes that the film propagandists in the early years of the Soviet Union were illustrating a noble ideal, however much it was betrayed in practice. But praise of Riefenstahl has no such recourse, since nobody, not even her rehabilitators, has managed to make Riefenstahl seem even likable; and she is no thinker at all.

More important, it is generally thought that National Socialism stands only for brutishness and terror. But this is not true. National Socialism—more broadly, fascism—also stands for an ideal or rather ideals that are persistent today under the other banners: the ideal of life as art, the cult of beauty, the fetishism of courage, the dissolution of alienation in ecstatic feelings of community; the repudiation of the intellect; the family of man (under the parenthood of leaders). These ideals are vivid and moving to many people, and it is dishonest as well as tautological to say that one is affected by *Triumph of the Will* and *Olympia* only because they were made by a filmmaker of genius. Riefenstahl's films are still effective because, among other reasons, their longings are still felt, because their content is a romantic ideal to which many continue to be attached and which is expressed in such diverse modes of cultural dissidence and propaganda for new forms of community as the youth/rock culture, primal therapy, anti-psychiatry, Third World camp-following, and belief in the occult. The exaltation of community does not preclude the search for absolute leadership; on the contrary, it may inevitably lead to it. (Not surprisingly, a fair number of the young people now prostrating themselves before gurus and submitting to the most grotesquely autocratic discipline are former anti-authoritarians and anti-elitists of the 1960s.)

Riefenstahl's current de-Nazification and vindication as indomitable priestess of the beautiful—as a filmmaker and, now, as a photographer—do not augur well for the keenness of current abilities to detect the fascist longings in our midst. Riefenstahl is hardly the usual sort of aesthete or anthropological romantic. The force of her work being precisely in the continuity of its political and aesthetic ideas, what is interesting is that this was once seen so much more clearly than it seems to be now, when people claim to be drawn to Riefenstahl's images for their beauty of composition. Without a historical perspective, such connoisseurship prepares the way for a curiously absentminded acceptance of propaganda for all sorts of destructive feelings—feelings whose implications people are refusing to take seriously. Somewhere, of course, everyone knows that more than beauty is at stake in art like Riefenstahl's. And so people hedge their bets—admiring this kind of art, for its undoubted beauty, and patronizing it, for its sanctimonious promotion of the beautiful. Backing up the solemn choosy formalist appreciations lies a larger reserve of appreciation, the sensibility of camp, which is unfettered by the scruples of high seriousness: and the modern sensibility relies on continuing trade-offs between the formalist approach and camp taste.

Art which evokes the themes of fascist aesthetic is popular now, and for most people it is probably no more than a variant of camp. Fascism may be merely fashionable, and perhaps fashion with its irrepressible promiscuity of taste will save us. But the judgments of taste themselves seem less innocent. Art that seemed eminently worth defending ten years ago, as a minority or adversary taste, no longer seems defensible today, because the ethical and cultural issues it raises have become serious, even dangerous, in a way they were not then. The hard truth is that what may be acceptable in elite culture may not be acceptable in mass culture, that tastes which pose only innocuous ethical issues as the property of a minority become corrupting when they become more established. Taste is context, and the context has changed.

II

Second Exhibit. Here is a book to be purchased at airport magazine stands and in "adult" bookstores, a relatively cheap paperback, not an expensive coffee-table item appealing to art lovers and the *bien-pensant* like *The Last of the Nuba*. Yet both books share a certain community of moral origin, a root preoccupation: the same preoccupation at different stages of evolution—the ideas that animate *The Last of the Nuba* being less out of the moral closet than the cruder, more efficient idea that lies behind *SS Regalia*. Though *SS Regalia* is a respectable British-made compilation (with a three-page historical preface and notes in the back), one knows that its appeal is not scholarly but sexual. The cover already makes that clear. Across the large black swastika of an SS armband is a diagonal yellow stripe which reads "Over 100 Brilliant Four-Color Photographs Only $2.95," exactly as a sticker with the price on it used to be affixed—part tease, part deference to censorship —on the cover of pornographic magazines, over the model's genitalia.

There is a general fantasy about uniforms. They suggest community, order, identity (through ranks, badges, medals, things which declare who the wearer is and what he has done: his worth is recognized), competence, legitimate authority, the legitimate exercise of violence. But uniforms are not the same thing as photographs of uniforms—which are erotic materials and photographs of SS uniforms are the units of a particularly powerful and widespread sexual fantasy. Why the SS? Because the SS was the ideal incarnation of fascism's overt assertion of the righteousness of violence, the right to have total power over others and to treat them as absolutely inferior. It was in the SS that this assertion seemed most complete, because they acted it out in a singularly brutal and efficient manner; and because they dramatized it by linking themselves to certain aesthetic standards. The SS was designed as an elite military community that would be not only supremely violent but also supremely beautiful. (One is not likely to come across a book called "SA Regalia." The SA, whom the SS replaced, were not known for being any less brutal than their successors, but they have gone down in history as beefy, squat, beerhall types; mere brownshirts.)

SS uniforms were stylish, well-cut, with a touch (but not too much) of eccentricity. Compare the rather boring and not very well cut American army uniform: jacket, shirt, tie, pants, socks, and lace-up shoes—essentially civilian clothes no matter how bedecked with medals and badges. SS uniforms were tight, heavy, stiff and included gloves to confine the hands and boots that made legs and feet feel heavy, encased, obliging their wearer to stand up straight. As the back cover of *SS Regalia* explains:

The uniform was black, a colour which had important overtones in Germany. On that, the SS wore a vast variety of decorations, symbols, badges to distinguish rank, from the collar runes to the death's-head. The appearance was both dramatic and menacing.

The cover's almost wistful come-on does not quite prepare one for the banality of most of the photographs. Along with those celebrated black uniforms, SS troopers were issued almost American-army-looking khaki uniforms and camouflage ponchos and jackets. And besides the photographs of uniforms, there are pages of collar patches, cuff bands, chevrons, belt buckles, commemorative badges, regimental standards, trumpet banners, field caps, service medals, shoulder flashes, permits, passes—few of which bear either the notorious runes or the death's-head; all meticulously identified by rank, unit, and year and season of issue. Precisely the innocuousness of practically all of the photographs testifies to the power of the image: one is handling the breviary of a sexual fantasy. For fantasy to have depth, it must have detail. What, for example, was the color of the travel permit an SS sergeant would have needed to get from Trier to Lübeck in the spring of 1944? One needs all the documentary evidence.

If the message of fascism has been neutralized by an aesthetic view of life, its trappings have been sexualized. This eroticization of fascism can be remarked in such enthralling and devout manifestations as Mishima's *Confessions of a Mask* and *Sun and Steel*, and in films like Kenneth Anger's *Scorpio Rising* and, more recently and far less interestingly, in Visconti's *The Damned* and Cavani's

The Night Porter. The solemn eroticizing of fascism must be distinguished from a sophisticated playing with cultural horror, where there is an element of the put-on. The poster Robert Morris made for his recent show at the Castelli Gallery is a photograph of the artist, naked to the waist, wearing dark glasses, what appears to be a Nazi helmet, and a spiked steel collar, attached to which is a stout chain which he holds in his manacled, uplifted hands. Morris is said to have considered this to be the only image that still has any power to shock: a singular virtue to those who take for granted that art is a sequence of ever-fresh gestures of provocation. But the point of the poster is its own negation. Shocking people in the context also means inuring them, as Nazi material enters the vast repertory of poular iconography usable for the ironic commentaries of Pop Art. Still, Nazism fascinates in a way other iconography staked out by the pop sensibility (from Mao Tse-tung to Marilyn Monroe) does not. No doubt, some part of the general rise of interest in fascism can be set down as a product of curiosity. For those born after the early 1940s, bludgeoned by a lifetime's palaver, pro and con, about communism, it is fascism—the great conversation piece of their parents' generation—which represents the exotic, the unknown. Then there is a general fascination among the young with horror, with the irrational. Courses dealing with the history of fascism are, along with those on the occult (including vampirism), among the best attended these days on college campuses. And beyond this the definitely sexual lure of fascism, which *SS Regalia* testifies to with unabashed plainness, seems impervious to deflation by irony or overfamiliarity.

In pornographic literature, films, and gadgetry throughout the world, especially in the United States, England, France, Japan, Scandinavia, Holland, and Germany, the SS has become a referent of sexual adventurism. Much of the imagery of far-out sex has been placed under the sign of Nazism. Boots, leather, chains, Iron Crosses on gleaming torsos, swastikas, along with meat hooks and heavy motorcycles, have become the secret and most lucrative paraphernalia of eroticism. In the sex shops, the baths, the leather bars, the brothels, people are dragging out their gear. But why? Why has Nazi Germany, which was a sexually repressive society, become erotic? How could a regime which persecuted homosexuals become a gay turn-on?

A clue lies in the predilections of the fascist leaders themselves for sexual metaphors. Like Nietzsche and Wagner, Hitler regarded leadership as sexual mastery of the "feminine" masses, as rape. (The expression of the crowds in *Triumph of the Will* is one of ecstasy; the leader makes the crowd come.) Left-wing movements have tended to be unisex, and asexual in their imagery. Right-wing movements, however puritanical and repressive the realities they usher in, have an erotic surface. Certainly Nazism is "sexier" than communism (which is not to the Nazis' credit, but rather shows something of the nature and limits of the sexual imagination).

Of course, most people who are turned on by SS uniforms are not signifying approval of what the Nazis did, if indeed they have more than the sketchiest idea of what that might be. Nevertheless, there are powerful and growing currents of sexual feeling, those that generally go by the name of sadomasochism, which make playing at Nazism seem erotic. These sadomasochistic fantasies and practices are to be found among heterosexuals as well as homosex-

uals, although it is among male homosexuals that the eroticizing of Nazism is most visible. S-m, not swinging, is the
big sexual secret of the last few years.

Between sadomasochism and fascism there is a natural
link. "Fascism is theater," as Genet said.* As is sadomasochistic sexuality: to be involved in sadomasochism is to
take part in a sexual theater, a staging of sexuality. Regulars of sadomasochistic sex are expert costumers and
choreographers as well as performers, in a drama that is all
the more exciting because it is forbidden to ordinary people. Sadomasochism is to sex what war is to civil life:
the magnificent experience. (Riefenstahl put it: "What is
purely realistic, slice of life, what is average, quotidian,
doesn't interest me." As the social contract seems tame in
comparison with war, so fucking and sucking come to seem

---

* It was Genet, in his novel *Funeral Rites*, who provided one of
the first texts that showed the erotic allure fascism exercised on
someone who was not a fascist. Another description is by Sartre,
an unlikely candidate for these feelings himself, who may have heard
about them from Genet. In *La Mort dans l'âme* (1949), the third
novel in his four-part *Les Chemins de la liberté*, Sartre describes one
of his protagonists experiencing the entry of the German army into
Paris in 1940: "[Daniel] was not afraid, he yielded trustingly to
those thousands of eyes, he thought 'Our conquerors!' and he was
supremely happy. He looked them in the eye, he feasted on their
fair hair, their sunburned faces with eyes which looked like lakes
of ice, their slim bodies, their incredibly long and muscular hips.
He murmured: 'How handsome they are!' . . . Something had fallen
from the sky: it was the ancient law. The society of judges had
collapsed, the sentence had been obliterated; those ghostly little
khaki soldiers, the defenders of the rights of man, had been routed.
. . . An unbearable, delicious sensation spread through his body; he
could hardly see properly; he repeated, gasping, 'As if it were
butter—they're entering Paris as if it were butter.' . . . He would
like to have been a woman to throw them flowers."

merely nice, and therefore unexciting. The end to which all sexual experience tends, as Bataille insisted in a lifetime of writing, is defilement, blasphemy. To be "nice," as to be civilized, means being alienated from this savage experience—which is entirely staged.

Sadomasochism, of course, does not just mean people hurting their sexual partners, which has always occurred—and generally means men beating up women. The perennial drunken Russian peasant thrashing his wife is just doing something he feels like doing (because he is unhappy, oppressed, stupefied; and because women are handy victims). But the perennial Englishman in a brothel being whipped is re-creating an experience. He is paying a whore to act out a piece of theater with him, to reenact or reevoke the past—experiences of his schooldays or nursery which now hold for him a huge reserve of sexual energy. Today it may be the Nazi past that people invoke, in the theatricalization of sexuality, because it is those images (rather than memories) from which they hope a reserve of sexual energy can be tapped. What the French call "the English vice" could, however, be said to be something of an artful affirmation of individuality; the playlet referred, after all, to the subject's own case history. The fad for Nazi regalia indicates something quite different: a response to an oppressive freedom of choice in sex (and in other matters), to an unbearable degree of individuality; the rehearsal of enslavement rather than its reenactment.

The rituals of domination and enslavement being more and more practiced, the art that is more and more devoted to rendering their themes, are perhaps only a logical extension of an affluent society's tendency to turn every part of people's lives into a taste, a choice; to invite them to regard their very lives as a (life) style. In all societies up to now, sex has mostly been an activity (something to do, without thinking about it). But once sex becomes a taste, it is perhaps already on its way to becoming a self-conscious form of theater, which is what sadomasochism is about: a form of gratification that is both violent and indirect, very mental.

Sadomasochism has always been the furthest reach of the sexual experience: when sex becomes most purely sexual, that is, severed from personhood, from relationships, from love. It should not be surprising that it has become attached to Nazi symbolism in recent years. Never before was the relation of masters and slaves so consciously aestheticized. Sade had to make up his theater of punishment and delight from scratch, improvising the decor and costumes and blasphemous rites. Now there is a master scenario available to everyone. The color is black, the material is leather, the seduction is beauty, the justification is honesty, the aim is ecstasy, the fantasy is death.

(1974)

Under the Sign
of Saturn

In most of the portrait photographs he is looking down, his right hand to his face. The earliest one I know shows him in 1927—he is thirty-five—with dark curly hair over a high forehead, mustache above a full lower lip: youthful, almost handsome. With his head lowered, his jacketed shoulders seem to start behind his ears; his thumb leans against his jaw; the rest of the hand, cigarette between bent index and third fingers, covers his chin; the downward look through his glasses—the soft, daydreamer's gaze of the myopic—seems to float off to the lower left of the photograph.

In a picture from the late 1930s, the curly hair has hardly receded, but there is no trace of youth or handsomeness; the face has widened and the upper torso seems not just high but blocky, huge. The thicker mustache and the pudgy folded hand with thumb tucked under cover his mouth. The look is opaque, or just more inward: he could be thinking—or listening. ("He who listens hard doesn't see," Benjamin wrote in his essay on Kafka.) There are books behind his head.

In a photograph taken in the summer of 1938, on the last of several visits he made to Brecht in exile in Denmark after 1933, he is standing in front of Brecht's house, an old man at forty-six, in white shirt, tie, trousers with watch chain: a slack, corpulent figure, looking truculently at the camera.

Another picture, from 1937, shows Benjamin in the Bibliothèque Nationale in Paris. Two men, neither of whose face can be seen, share a table some distance behind him. Benjamin sits in the right foreground, probably taking notes for the book on Baudelaire and nineteenth-century Paris he had been writing for a decade. He is consulting a volume he holds open on the table with his left hand—his eyes can't be seen—looking, as it were, into the lower right edge of the photograph.

His close friend Gershom Scholem has described his first glimpse of Benjamin in Berlin in 1913, at a joint meeting of a Zionist youth group and Jewish members of the Free German Student Association, of which the twenty-one-year-old Benjamin was a leader. He spoke "extempore without so much as a glance at his audience, staring with a fixed gaze at a remote corner of the ceiling which he harangued with much intensity, in a style incidentally that was, as far as I remember, ready for print."

He was what the French call *un triste*. In his youth he seemed marked by "a profound sadness," Scholem wrote.

Under the Sign of Saturn

He thought of himself as a melancholic, disdaining modern psychological labels and invoking the traditional astrological one: "I came into the world under the sign of Saturn—the star of the slowest revolution, the planet of detours and delays. . . ." His major projects, the book published in 1928 on the German baroque drama (the *Trauerspiel*; literally, sorrow-play) and his never completed *Paris, Capital of the Nineteenth Century*, cannot be fully understood unless one grasps how much they rely on a theory of melancholy.

Benjamin projected himself, his temperament, into all his major subjects, and his temperament determined what he chose to write about. It was what he saw in subjects, such as the seventeenth-century baroque plays (which dramatize different facets of "Saturnine acedia") and the writers about whose work he wrote most brilliantly—Baudelaire, Proust, Kafka, Karl Kraus. He even found the Saturnine element in Goethe. For, despite the polemic in his great (still untranslated) essay on Goethe's *Elective Affinities* against interpreting a writer's work by his life, he did make selective use of the life in his deepest meditations on texts: information that disclosed the melancholic, the solitary. (Thus, he describes Proust's "loneliness which pulls the world down into its vortex"; explains how Kafka, like Klee, was "essentially solitary"; cites Robert Walser's "horror of success in life.") One cannot use the life to interpret the work. But one can use the work to interpret the life.

Two short books of reminiscences of his Berlin childhood and student years, written in the early 1930s and unpublished in his lifetime, contain Benjamin's most explicit self-portrait. To the nascent melancholic, in school and on walks with his mother, "solitude appeared to me as the only fit state of man." Benjamin does not mean solitude in a room—he was often sick as a child—but solitude in the great metropolis, the busyness of the idle stroller, free to daydream, observe, ponder, cruise. The mind who was to attach much of the nineteenth century's sensibility to the figure of the *flâneur*, personified by that superbly self-aware melancholic Baudelaire, spun much of his own sensibility out of his phantasmagorical, shrewd, subtle relation to cities. The street, the passage, the arcade, the labyrinth are recurrent themes in his literary essays and, notably, in the projected book on nineteenth-century Paris, as well as in his travel pieces and reminiscences. (Robert Walser, for whom walking was the center of his reclusive life and marvelous books, is a writer to whom one particularly wishes Benjamin had devoted a longer essay.) The only book of a discreetly autobiographical nature published in his lifetime was titled *One-Way Street*. Reminiscences of self are reminiscences of a place, and how he positions himself in it, navigates around it.

"Not to find one's way about in a city is of little interest," begins his still untranslated *A Berlin Childhood Around the Turn of the Century*. "But to lose one's way in a city, as one loses one's way in a forest, requires practice. . . . I learned this art late in life: it fulfilled the dreams whose first traces were the labyrinths on the blotters of my exercise books." This passage also occurs in *A Berlin Chronicle*, after Benjamin suggests how much practice it took to get lost, given an original sense of "impotence before the city." His goal is to be a competent street-map reader who knows how to stray. And to locate himself, with imaginary maps. Elsewhere in *Berlin Chronicle* Benjamin relates that for years he had played with the idea of mapping his life. For this map, which he imagined as gray, he had devised a

colorful system of signs that "clearly marked in the houses
of my friends and girl friends, the assembly halls of various
collectives, from the 'debating chambers' of the Youth
Movement to the gathering places of the Communist youth,
the hotel and brothel rooms that I knew for one night, the
decisive benches in the Tiergarten, the ways to different
schools and the graves that I saw filled, the sites of presti-
gious cafés whose long-forgotten names daily crossed our
lips." Once, waiting for someone in the Café des Deux
Magots in Paris, he relates, he managed to draw a diagram
of his life: it was like a labyrinth, in which each important
relationship figures as "an entrance to the maze."

The recurrent metaphors of maps and diagrams, memories and dreams, labyrinths and arcades, vistas and pan-
oramas, evoke a certain vision of cities as well as a certain
kind of life. Paris, Benjamin writes, "taught me the art of
straying." The revelation of the city's true nature came not
in Berlin but in Paris, where he stayed frequently throughout the Weimar years, and lived as a refugee from 1933
until his suicide while trying to escape from France in 1940
—more exactly, the Paris reimagined in the Surrealist narratives (Breton's *Nadja*, Aragon's *Le Paysan de Paris*).
With these metaphors, he is indicating a general problem
about orientation, and erecting a standard of difficulty and
complexity. (A labyrinth is a place where one gets lost.)
He is also suggesting a notion about the forbidden, and how
to gain access to it: through an act of the mind that is the
same as a physical act. "Whole networks of streets were
opened up under the auspices of prostitution," he writes in
Berlin Chronicle, which begins by invoking an Ariadne, the
whore who leads this son of rich parents for the first time
across "the threshold of class." The metaphor of the

labyrinth also suggests Benjamin's idea of obstacles thrown up by his own temperament.

The influence of Saturn makes people "apathetic, indecisive, slow," he writes in *The Origin of German Trauerspiel* (1928). Slowness is one characteristic of the melancholic temperament. Blundering is another, from noticing too many possibilities, from not noticing one's lack of practical sense. And stubbornness, from the longing to be superior— on one's own terms. Benjamin recalls his stubbornness during childhood walks with his mother, who would turn insignificant items of conduct into tests of his aptitude for practical life, thereby reinforcing what was inept ("my inability even today to make a cup of coffee") and dreamily recalcitrant in his nature. "My habit of seeming slower, more maladroit, more stupid than I am, had its origin in such walks, and has the great attendant danger of making me think myself quicker, more dexterous, and shrewder than I am." And from this stubbornness comes, "above all, a gaze that appears to see not a third of what it takes in."

One-Way Street distills the experiences of the writer and lover (it is dedicated to Asja Lacis, who "cut it through the author"),* experiences that can be guessed at in the opening words on the writer's situation, which sound the theme of revolutionary moralism, and the final "To the Plane-

---

* Asja Lacis and Benjamin met in Capri in the summer of 1924. She was a Latvian Communist revolutionary and theater director, assistant to Brecht and to Piscator, with whom Benjamin wrote "Naples" in 1925 and for whom he wrote "Program for a Proletarian Children's Theater" in 1928. It was Lacis who got Benjamin an invitation to Moscow in the winter of 1926–27 and who introduced him to Brecht in 1929. Benjamin hoped to marry her when he and his wife were finally divorced in 1930. But she returned to Riga and later spent ten years in a Soviet camp.

tarium," a paean to the technological wooing of nature and to sexual ecstasy. Benjamin could write about himself more directly when he started from memories, not contemporary experiences; when he writes about himself as a child. At that distance, childhood, he can survey his life as a space that can be mapped. The candor and the surge of painful feelings in *Berlin Childhood* and *Berlin Chronicle* become possible precisely because Benjamin has adopted a completely digested, analytical way of relating the past. It evokes events for the reactions to the events, places for the emotions one has deposited in the places, other people for the encounter with oneself, feelings and behavior for intimations of future passions and failures contained in them. Fantasies of monsters loose in the large apartment while his parents entertain their friends prefigure his revulsion against his class; the dream of being allowed to sleep as long as he wants, instead of having to get up early to go to school, will be fulfilled when—after his book on the *Trauerspiel* failed to qualify him for a university lectureship—he realizes that "his hopes of a position and a secure livelihood had always been in vain"; his way of walking with his mother, "with pedantic care" keeping one step behind her, prefigures his "sabotage of real social existence."

Benjamin regards everything he chooses to recall in his past as prophetic of the future, because the work of memory (reading oneself backward, he called it) collapses time. There is no chronological ordering of his reminiscences, for which he disavows the name of autobiography, because time is irrelevant. ("Autobiography has to do with time, with sequence and what makes up the continuous flow of life," he writes in *Berlin Chronicle*. "Here, I am talking of a space, of moments and discontinuities.") Benjamin, the translator of Proust, wrote fragments of an opus that could be called *A la recherche des espaces perdus*. Memory, the staging of the past, turns the flow of events into tableaux. Benjamin is not trying to recover his past but to understand it: to condense it into its spatial forms, its premonitory structures.

For the baroque dramatists, he writes in *The Origin of German Trauerspiel*, "chronological movement is grasped and analyzed in a spatial image." The book on the *Trauerspiel* is not only Benjamin's first account of what it means to convert time into space; it is where he explains most clearly what feeling underlies this move. Awash in melancholic awareness of "the disconsolate chronicle of world history," a process of incessant decay, the baroque dramatists seek to escape from history and restore the "timelessness" of paradise. The seventeenth-century baroque sensibility had a "panoramatic" conception of history: "history merges into the setting." In *Berlin Childhood* and *Berlin Chronicle*, Benjamin merges his life into a setting. The successor to the baroque stage set is the Surrealist city: the metaphysical landscape in whose dreamlike spaces people have "a brief, shadowy existence," like the nineteen-year-old poet whose suicide, the great sorrow of Benjamin's student years, is condensed in the memory of rooms that the dead friend inhabited.

Benjamin's recurrent themes are, characteristically, means of spatializing the world: for example, his notion of ideas and experiences as ruins. To understand something is to understand its topography, to know how to chart it. And to know how to get lost.

For the character born under the sign of Saturn, time is the medium of constraint, inadequacy, repetition, mere fulfillment. In time, one is only what one is: what one has always been. In space, one can be another person. Benjamin's poor sense of direction and inability to read a street map become his love of travel and his mastery of the art of straying. Time does not give one much leeway: it thrusts us forward from behind, blows us through the narrow funnel of the present into the future. But space is broad, teeming with possibilities, positions, intersections, passages, detours, U-turns, dead ends, one-way streets. Too many possibilities, indeed. Since the Saturnine temperament is slow, prone to indecisiveness, sometimes one has to cut one's way through with a knife. Sometimes one ends by turning the knife against oneself.

The mark of the Saturnine temperament is the self-conscious and unforgiving relation to the self, which can never be taken for granted. The self is a text—it has to be deciphered. (Hence, this is an apt temperament for intellectuals.) The self is a project, something to be built. (Hence, this is an apt temperament for artists and martyrs, those who court "the purity and beauty of a failure," as Benjamin says of Kafka.) And the process of building a self and its works is always too slow. One is always in arrears to oneself.

Things appear at a distance, come forward slowly. In *Berlin Childhood*, he speaks of his "propensity for seeing everything I care about approach me from far away"—the way, often ill as a child, he imagined the hours approaching his sickbed. "This is perhaps the origin of what others call patience in me, but which in truth does not resemble any virtue." (Of course, others did experience it as patience, as a virtue. Scholem has described him as "the most patient human being I ever came to know.")

But something like patience is needed for the melancholic's labors of decipherment. Proust, as Benjamin notes, was excited by "the secret language of the salons"; Benjamin was drawn to more compact codes. He collected emblem books, liked to make up anagrams, played with pseudonyms. His taste for pseudonyms well antedates his need as a German-Jewish refugee, who from 1933 to 1936 continued to publish reviews in German magazines under the name of Detlev Holz, the name he used to sign the last book to appear in his lifetime, *Deutsche Menschen*, published in Switzerland in 1936. In the amazing text written in Ibiza in 1933, "Agesilaus Santander," Benjamin speaks of his fantasy of having a secret name; the name of this text—which turns on the figure in the Klee drawing he owned, "Angelus Novus"—is, as Scholem has pointed out, an anagram of *Der Angelus Santanas*. He was an "uncanny" graphologist, Scholem reports, though "later on he tended to conceal his gift."

Dissimulation, secretiveness appear a necessity to the melancholic. He has complex, often veiled relations with others. These feelings of superiority, of inadequacy, of baffled feeling, of not being able to get what one wants, or even name it properly (or consistently) to oneself—these can be, it is felt they ought to be, masked by friendliness, or the most scrupulous manipulation. Using a word that was also applied to Kafka by those who knew him, Scholem speaks of "the almost Chinese courtesy" that characterized Benjamin's relations with people. But one is not surprised to learn, of the man who could justify Proust's "invectives against friendship," that Benjamin could also drop friends brutally, as he did his comrades from the Youth Movement, when they no longer interested him. Nor is one surprised to learn that this fastidious, intransigent, fiercely serious man could also flatter people he probably did not think his equals, that he could let himself be "baited" (his own word) and condescended to by Brecht on his visits to Denmark. This prince of the intellectual life could also be a courtier.

Benjamin analyzed both roles in *The Origin of German Trauerspiel* by the theory of melancholy. One characteristic of the Saturnine temperament is slowness: "The tyrant falls on account of the sluggishness of his emotions." "Another trait of the predominance of Saturn," says Benjamin, is "faithlessness." This is represented by the character of the courtier in baroque drama, whose mind is "fluctuation itself." The manipulativeness of the courtier is partly a "lack of character"; partly it "reflects an inconsolable, despondent surrender to an impenetrable conjunction of baleful constellations [that] seem to have taken on a massive, almost thing-like cast." Only someone identifying with this sense of historical catastrophe, this degree of despondency, would have explained why the courtier is not to be despised. His faithlessness to his fellow men, Benjamin says, corresponds to the "deeper, more contemplative faith" he keeps with material emblems.

What Benjamin describes could be understood as simple pathology: the tendency of the melancholic temperament to project its inner torpor outward, as the immutability of misfortune, which is experienced as "massive, almost thing-like." But his argument is more daring: he perceives that the deep transactions between the melancholic and the world always take place with things (rather than with people); and that these are genuine transactions, which reveal meaning. Precisely because the melancholy character is haunted by death, it is melancholics who best know how to read the world. Or, rather, it is the world which yields itself to the melancholic's scrutiny, as it does to no one else's. The more lifeless things are, the more potent and ingenious can be the mind which contemplates them.

If this melancholy temperament is faithless to people, it has good reason to be faithful to things. Fidelity lies in accumulating things—which appear, mostly, in the form of fragments or ruins. ("It is common practice in baroque literature to pile up fragments incessantly," Benjamin writes.) Both the baroque and Surrealism, sensibilities with which Benjamin felt a strong affinity, see reality as things. Benjamin describes the baroque as a world of things (emblems, ruins) and spatialized ideas ("Allegories are, in the realm of thought, what ruins are in the realm of things"). The genius of Surrealism was to generalize with ebullient candor the baroque cult of ruins; to perceive that the nihilistic energies of the modern era make everything a ruin or fragment—and therefore collectible. A world whose past has become (by definition) obsolete, and whose present churns out instant antiques, invites custodians, decoders, and collectors.

As one kind of collector himself, Benjamin remained faithful to things—as things. According to Scholem, building his library, which included many first editions and rare books, was "his most enduring personal passion." Inert in the face of thing-like disaster, the melancholy temperament is galvanized by the passions aroused by privileged objects. Benjamin's books were not only for use, professional tools; they were contemplative objects, stimuli for reverie. His library evokes "memories of the cities in which I found so many things: Riga, Naples, Munich, Danzig, Moscow, Florence, Basel, Paris . . . memories of the rooms where these books had been housed. . . ." Bookhunting, like the sexual hunt, adds to the geography of pleasure—another reason for strolling about in the world. In collecting, Benjamin experienced what in himself was clever, successful, shrewd, unabashedly passionate. "Collectors are people with a tactical instinct"—like courtiers.

Apart from first editions and baroque emblem books, Benjamin specialized in children's books and books written by the mad. "The great works which meant so much to him," reports Scholem, "were placed in bizarre patterns next to the most out-of-the-way writings and oddities." The odd arrangement of the library is like the strategy of Benjamin's work, in which a Surrealist-inspired eye for the treasures of meaning in the ephemeral, discredited, and neglected worked in tandem with his loyalty to the traditional canon of learned taste.

He liked finding things where nobody was looking. He drew from the obscure, disdained German baroque drama elements of the modern (that is to say, his own) sensibility: the taste for allegory, Surrealist shock effects, discontinuous utterance, the sense of historical catastrophe. "These stones were the bread of my imagination," he wrote about Marseilles—the most recalcitrant of cities to that imagination, even when helped by a dose of hashish. Many expected references are absent in Benjamin's work —he didn't like to read what everybody was reading. He preferred the doctrine of the four temperaments as a psychological theory to Freud. He preferred being a communist, or trying to be one, without reading Marx. This man who read virtually everything, and had spent fifteen years sympathizing with revolutionary communism, had barely looked into Marx until the late 1930s. (He was reading *The Eighteenth Brumaire* on his visit to Brecht in Denmark in the summer of 1938.)

His sense of strategy was one of his points of identification with Kafka, a kindred would-be tactician, who "took precautions against the interpretation of his writing." The whole point of the Kafka stories, Benjamin argues, is that they have *no* definite, symbolic meaning. And he was fascinated by the very different, un-Jewish sense of ruse practiced by Brecht, the anti-Kafka of his imagination. (Predictably, Brecht disliked Benjamin's great essay on Kafka intensely.) Brecht, with the little wooden donkey near his desk from whose neck hung the sign "I, too, must understand it," represented for Benjamin, an admirer of esoteric religious texts, the possibly more potent ruse of reducing complexity, of making everything clear. Benjamin's "masochistic" (the word is Siegfried Kracauer's) relation to Brecht, which most of his friends deplored, shows the extent to which he was fascinated by this possibility.

Benjamin's propensity is to go against the usual interpretation. "All the decisive blows are struck left-handed," as he says in *One-Way Street*. Precisely because he saw that "all human knowledge takes the form of interpretation," he understood the importance of being against interpretation wherever it is obvious. His most common strategy is to drain symbolism out of some things, like the Kafka stories or Goethe's *Elective Affinities* (texts where everybody agrees it is there), and pour it into others, where nobody suspects its existence (such as the German baroque plays, which he reads as allegories of historical pessimism). "Each book is a tactic," he wrote. In a letter to a friend, he claimed for his writings, only partly facetiously, forty-nine levels of meaning. For moderns as much as for cabalists,

nothing is straightforward. Everything is—at the least—
difficult. "Ambiguity displaces authenticity in all things,"
he wrote in *One-Way Street*. What is most foreign to Benjamin is anything like ingenuousness: "the 'unclouded,'
'innocent' eye has become a lie."

Much of the originality of Benjamin's arguments owes
to his microscopic gaze (as his friend and disciple Theodor
Adorno called it), combined with his indefatigable command over theoretical perspectives. "It was the small
things that attracted him most," writes Scholem. He loved
old toys, postage stamps, picture postcards, and such playful miniaturizations of reality as the winter world inside a
glass globe that snows when it is shaken. His own handwriting was almost microscopic, and his never realized
ambition, Scholem reports, was to get a hundred lines on a
sheet of paper. (The ambition was realized by Robert
Walser, who used to transcribe the manuscripts of his stories and novels as micrograms, in a truly microscopic
script.) Scholem relates that when he visited Benjamin in
Paris in August 1927 (the first time the two friends had
seen each other since Scholem emigrated to Palestine in
1923), Benjamin dragged him to an exhibit of Jewish ritual objects at the Musée Cluny to show him "two grains of
wheat on which a kindred soul had inscribed the complete
Shema Israel."*

* Scholem argues that Benjamin's love for the miniature underlies
his taste for brief literary utterances, evident in *One-Way Street*.
Perhaps; but books of this sort were common in the 1920s, and it was
in a specifically Surrealist montage style that these short independent
texts were presented. *One-Way Street* was published by Ernst Rowohlt
in Berlin, in booklet form with typography intended to evoke advertising shock effects; the cover was a photographic montage of
aggressive phrases in capital letters from newspaper announcements,

To miniaturize is to make portable—the ideal form of possessing things for a wanderer, or a refugee. Benjamin, of course, was both a wanderer, on the move, and a collector, weighed down by things; that is, passions. To miniaturize is to conceal. Benjamin was drawn to the extremely small as he was to whatever had to be deciphered: emblems, anagrams, handwriting. To miniaturize means to make useless. For what is so grotesquely reduced is, in a sense, liberated from its meaning—its tininess being the outstanding thing about it. It is both a whole (that is, complete) and a fragment (so tiny, the wrong scale). It becomes an object of disinterested contemplation or reverie. Love of the small is a child's emotion, one colonized by Surrealism. The Paris of the Surrealists is "a little world," Benjamin observes; so is the photograph, which Surrealist taste discovered as an enigmatic, even perverse, rather than a merely intelligible or beautiful, object, and about which Benjamin wrote with such originality. The melancholic always feels threatened by the dominion of the thing-like, but Surrealist taste mocks these terrors. Surrealism's great gift to sensibility was to make melancholy cheerful.

"The only pleasure the melancholic permits himself, and it is a powerful one, is allegory," Benjamin wrote in *The Origin of German Trauerspiel*. Indeed, he asserted, allegory is the way of reading the world typical of melancholics, and quoted Baudelaire: "Everything for me becomes Allegory." The process which extracts meaning

---

ads, official and odd signs. The opening passage, in which Benjamin hails "prompt language" and denounces "the pretentious, universal gesture of the book," does not make much sense unless one knows what kind of book *One-Way Street* was designed to be.

from the petrified and insignificant, allegory, is the characteristic method of the German baroque drama and of Baudelaire, Benjamin's major subjects; and, transmuted into philosophical argument and the micrological analysis of things, the method Benjamin practiced himself.

The melancholic sees the world itself become a thing: refuge, solace, enchantment. Shortly before his death, Benjamin was planning an essay about miniaturization as a device of fantasy. It seems to have been a continuation of an old plan to write on Goethe's "The New Melusina" (in *Wilhelm Meister*), which is about a man who falls in love with a woman who is actually a tiny person, temporarily granted normal size, and unknowingly carries around with him a box containing the miniature kingdom of which she is the princess. In Goethe's tale, the world is reduced to a collectible thing, an object, in the most literal sense.

Like the box in Goethe's tale, a book is not only a fragment of the world but itself a little world. The book is a miniaturization of the world, which the reader inhabits. In *Berlin Chronicle*, Benjamin evokes his childhood rapture: "You did not read books through; you dwelt, abided between their lines." To reading, the delirium of the child, was eventually added writing, the obsession of the adult. The most praiseworthy way of acquiring books is by writing them, Benjamin remarks in an essay called "Unpacking My Library." And the best way to understand them is also to enter their space: one never really understands a book unless one copies it, he says in *One-Way Street*, as one never understands a landscape from an airplane but only by walking through it.

"The amount of meaning is in exact proportion to the presence of death and the power of decay," Benjamin writes in the *Trauerspiel* book. This is what makes it possible to find meaning in one's own life, in "the dead occurrences of the past which are euphemistically known as experience." Only because the past is dead is one able to read it. Only because history is fetishized in physical objects can one understand it. Only because the book is a world can one enter it. The book for him was another space in which to stroll. For the character born under the sign of Saturn, the true impulse when one is being looked at is to cast down one's eyes, look in a corner. Better, one can lower one's head to one's notebook. Or put one's head behind the wall of a book.

It is characteristic of the Saturnine temperament to blame its undertow of inwardness on the will. Convinced that the will is weak, the melancholic may make extravagant efforts to develop it. If these efforts are successful, the resulting hypertrophy of will usually takes the form of a compulsive devotion to work. Thus Baudelaire, who suffered constantly from "acedia, the malady of monks," ended many letters and his *Intimate Journals* with the most impassioned pledges to work more, to work uninterruptedly, to do nothing but work. (Despair over "every defeat of the will"— Baudelaire's phrase again—is a characteristic complaint of modern artists and intellectuals, particularly of those who are both.) One is condemned to work; otherwise, one might not do anything at all. Even the dreaminess of the melancholic temperament is harnessed to work, and the melancholic may try to cultivate phantasmagorical states, like dreams, or seek the access to concentrated states of attention offered by drugs. Surrealism simply puts a positive accent on what Baudelaire experienced so negatively: it does not deplore the guttering of volition but raises it to an ideal, proposing that dream states may be relied on to furnish all the material needed for work.

Benjamin, always working, always trying to work more, speculated a good deal on the writer's daily existence. *One-Way Street* has several sections which offer recipes for work: the best conditions, timing, utensils. Part of the impetus for the large correspondence he conducted was to chronicle, report on, confirm the existence of work. His instincts as a collector served him well. Learning was a form of collecting, as in the quotations and excerpts from daily reading which Benjamin accumulated in notebooks that he carried everywhere and from which he would read aloud to friends. Thinking was also a form of collecting, at least in its preliminary stages. He conscientiously logged stray ideas; developed mini-essays in letters to friends; re-wrote plans for future projects; noted his dreams (several are recounted in *One-Way Street*); kept numbered lists of all the books he read. (Scholem recalls seeing, on his second and last visit to Benjamin in Paris, in 1938, a notebook of current reading in which Marx's *Eighteenth Brumaire* is listed as No. 1649.)

How does the melancholic become a hero of will? Through the fact that work can become like a drug, a compulsion. ("Thinking which is an eminent narcotic," he wrote in the essay on Surrealism.) In fact, melancholics make the best addicts, for the true addictive experience is always a solitary one. The hashish sessions of the late 1920s, supervised by a doctor friend, were prudent stunts, not acts of self-surrender; material for the writer, not escape from the exactions of the will. (Benjamin considered the book he wanted to write on hashish one of his most important projects.)

The need to be solitary—along with bitterness over

one's loneliness—is characteristic of the melancholic. To get work done, one must be solitary—or, at least, not bound to any permanent relationship. Benjamin's negative feelings about marriage are clear in the essay on Goethe's *Elective Affinities*. His heroes—Kierkegaard, Baudelaire, Proust, Kafka, Kraus—never married; and Scholem reports that Benjamin came to regard his own marriage (he was married in 1917, estranged from his wife after 1921, and divorced in 1930) "as fatal to himself." The world of nature, and of natural relationships, is perceived by the melancholic temperament as less than seductive. The self-portrait in *Berlin Childhood* and *Berlin Chronicle* is of a wholly alienated son; as husband and father (he had a son, born in 1918, who emigrated to England with Benjamin's ex-wife in the mid-1930s), he appears to have simply not known what to do with these relationships. For the melancholic, the natural, in the form of family ties, introduces the falsely subjective, the sentimental; it is a drain on the will, on one's independence; on one's freedom to concentrate on work. It also presents a challenge to one's humanity to which the melancholic knows, in advance, he will be inadequate.

The style of work of the melancholic is immersion, total concentration. Either one is immersed, or attention floats away. As a writer, Benjamin was capable of extraordinary concentration. He was able to research and write *The Origin of German Trauerspiel* in two years; some of it, he boasts in *Berlin Chronicle*, was written in long evenings at a café, sitting close to a jazz band. But although Benjamin wrote prolifically—in some periods turning out work every week for the German literary papers and magazines—it proved impossible for him to write a normal-sized book again. In a letter in 1935, Benjamin speaks of "the Saturnine pace" of writing *Paris, Capital of the Nineteenth Century*, which he had begun in 1927 and thought could be finished in two years. His characteristic form remained the essay. The melancholic's intensity and exhaustiveness of attention set natural limits to the length at which Benjamin could develop his ideas. His major essays seem to end just in time, before they self-destruct.

His sentences do not seem to be generated in the usual way; they do not entail. Each sentence is written as if it were the first, or the last. ("A writer must stop and restart with every new sentence," he says in the Prologue to *The Origin of German Trauerspiel*.) Mental and historical processes are rendered as conceptual tableaux; ideas are transcribed in extremis and the intellectual perspectives are vertiginous. His style of thinking and writing, incorrectly called aphoristic, might better be called freeze-frame baroque. This style was torture to execute. It was as if each sentence had to say everything, before the inward gaze of total concentration dissolved the subject before his eyes. Benjamin was probably not exaggerating when he told Adorno that each idea in his book on Baudelaire and nineteenth-century Paris "had to be wrested away from a realm in which madness lies."*

Something like the dread of being stopped prematurely lies behind these sentences as saturated with ideas as the surface of a baroque painting is jammed with movement.

---

* In a letter from Adorno to Benjamin, written from New York on November 10, 1938. Benjamin and Adorno met in 1923 (Adorno was twenty), and in 1935 Benjamin started to receive a small stipend from Max Horkheimer's Institut für Sozialforschung, of which Adorno was a member.

In a letter to Adorno in 1935, Benjamin describes his transports when he first read Aragon's *Le Paysan de Paris*, the book that inspired *Paris, Capital of the Nineteenth Century*: "I would never read more than two or three pages in bed of an evening because the pounding of my heart was so loud that I had to let the book fall from my hands. What a warning!" Cardiac failure is the metaphoric limit of Benjamin's exertions and passions. (He suffered from a heart ailment.) And cardiac sufficiency is a metaphor he offers for the writer's achievement. In the essay in praise of Karl Kraus, Benjamin writes:

> If style is the power to move freely in the length and breadth of linguistic thinking without falling into banality, it is attained chiefly by the cardiac strength of great thoughts, which drives the blood of language through the capillaries of syntax into the remotest limbs.

Thinking, writing are ultimately questions of stamina. The melancholic, who feels he lacks will, may feel that he needs all the destructive energies he can muster.

"Truth resists being projected into the realm of knowledge," Benjamin writes in *The Origin of German Trauerspiel*. His dense prose registers that resistance, and leaves no space for attacking those who distribute lies. Benjamin considered polemic beneath the dignity of a truly philosophical style, and sought instead what he called "the fullness of concentrated positivity"—the essay on Goethe's *Elective Affinities*, with its devastating refutation of the critic and Goethe biographer Friedrich Gundolf, being the one exception to this rule among his major writings. But his awareness of the ethical utility of polemic made him appreciate that one-man Viennese public institution, Karl Kraus, a writer whose facility, stridency, love of the a-phoristic, and indefatigable polemic energies make him so unlike Benjamin.

The essay on Kraus is Benjamin's most passionate and perverse defense of the life of the mind. "The perfidious reproach of being 'too intelligent' haunted him through-out his life," Adorno has written. Benjamin defended him-self against this philistine defamation by bravely raising the standard of the "inhumanity" of the intellect, when it is properly—that is, ethically—employed. "The life of let-ters is existence under the aegis of mere mind as prostitu-tion is existence under the aegis of mere sexuality," he wrote. This is to celebrate both prostitution (as Kraus did, because mere sexuality was sexuality in a pure state) and the life of letters, as Benjamin did, using the unlikely fig-ure of Kraus, because of "the genuine and demonic func-tion of mere mind, to be a disturber of the peace." The ethical task of the modern writer is to be not a creator but a destroyer—a destroyer of shallow inwardness, the consol-ing notion of the universally human, dilettantish creativ-ity, and empty phrases.

The writer as scourge and destroyer, portrayed in the figure of Kraus, he sketched with concision and even greater boldness in the allegorical "The Destructive Char-acter," also written in 1931. Scholem has written that the first of several times Benjamin contemplated suicide was in the summer of 1931. The second time was the following summer, when he wrote "Agesilaus Santander." The Apol-lonian scourge whom Benjamin calls the destructive char-acter

is always blithely at work ... has few needs ... has
no interest in being understood . . . is young and
cheerful . . . and feels not that life is worth living
but that suicide is not worth the trouble.

It is a kind of conjuration, an attempt by Benjamin to
draw the destructive elements of his Saturnine character
outward—so that they are not self-destructive.

Benjamin is not referring just to his own destructiveness. He thought that there was a peculiarly modern
temptation to suicide. In "The Paris of the Second Empire
in Baudelaire," he wrote:

> The resistance which modernity offers to the
> natural productive élan of a person is out of propor-
> tion to his strength. It is understandable if a person
> grows tired and takes refuge in death. Modernity
> must be under the sign of suicide, an act which
> seals a heroic will. . . . It is *the* achievement of
> modernity in the realm of passions. . . .

Suicide is understood as a response of the heroic will to the
defeat of the will. The only way to avoid suicide, Benjamin
suggests, is to be beyond heroism, beyond efforts of the
will. The destructive character cannot feel trapped, because "he sees ways everywhere." Cheerfully engaged in
reducing what exists to rubble, he "positions himself at the
crossroads."

Benjamin's portrait of the destructive character would
evoke a kind of Siegfried of the mind—a high-spirited,
childlike brute under the protection of the gods—had this
apocalyptic pessimism not been qualified by the irony al-

ways within the range of the Saturnine temperament. Irony is the positive name which the melancholic gives to his solitude, his asocial choices. In *One-Way Street* Benjamin hailed the irony that allows individuals to assert the right to lead lives independent of the community as "the most European of all accomplishments," and observed that it had completely deserted Germany. Benjamin's taste for the ironic and the self-aware put him off most of recent German culture: he detested Wagner, despised Heidegger, and scorned the frenetic vanguard movements of Weimar Germany such as Expressionism.

Passionately, but also ironically, Benjamin placed himself at the crossroads. It was important for him to keep his many "positions" open: the theological, the Surrealist/ aesthetic, the communist. One position corrects another; he needed them all. Decisions, of course, tended to spoil the balance of these positions, vacillation kept everything in place. The reason he gave for his delay in leaving France, when he last saw Adorno in early 1938, was that "there are still positions here to defend."

Benjamin thought the freelance intellectual was a dying species anyway, made no less obsolete by capitalist society than by revolutionary communism; indeed, he felt that he was living in a time in which everything valuable was the last of its kind. He thought Surrealism was the last intelligent moment of the European intelligentsia, an appropriately destructive, nihilistic kind of intelligence. In his essay on Kraus, Benjamin asks rhetorically: Does Kraus stand on the frontier of a new age? "Alas, by no means. For he stands on the threshold of the Last Judgment." Benjamin is thinking of himself. At the Last Judgment, the Last Intellectual—that Saturnine hero of modern culture, with his ruins, his defiant visions, his reveries, his unquenchable gloom, his downcast eyes—will explain that he took many "positions" and defended the life of the mind to the end, as righteously and inhumanly as he could.

(1978)

Syberberg's Hitler

Wer nicht von dreitausend Jahren
Sich weiss Rechenschaft zu geben
Bleib im Dunkeln, unerfahren,
Mag von Tag zu Tage leben.

—GOETHE

[Anyone who cannot give an account
to oneself of the past three thousand
years remains in darkness, without
experience, living from day to day.]

The Romantics thought of great art as a species of heroism, a breaking through or going beyond. Following them,
adepts of the modern demanded of masterpieces that they
be, in each case, an extreme case—terminal or prophetic,
or both. Walter Benjamin was making a characteristic
modernist judgment when he observed (writing about
Proust): "All great works of literature found a genre or
dissolve one." However rich in precursors, the truly great
work must seem to break with an old order and really is a
devastating if salutary move. Such a work extends the
reach of art but also complicates and burdens the enterprise of art with new, self-conscious standards. It both ex-
cites and paralyzes the imagination.

Lately, the appetite for the truly great work has become
less robust. Thus Hans-Jürgen Syberberg's *Hitler, a Film*

from Germany is not only daunting because of the extremity of its achievement, but discomfiting, like an unwanted baby in the era of zero population growth. The modernism that reckoned achievement by the Romantics' grandiose aims for art (as wisdom/as salvation/as cultural subversion or revolution) has been overtaken by an impudent version of itself which has enabled modernist tastes to be diffused on an undreamed-of scale. Stripped of its heroic stature, of its claims as an adversary sensibility, modernism has proved acutely compatible with the ethos of an advanced consumer society. Art is now the name of a huge variety of satisfactions—of the unlimited proliferation, and devaluation, of satisfaction itself. Where so many blandishments flourish, bringing off a masterpiece seems a retrograde feat, a naïve form of accomplishment. Always implausible (as implausible as justified megalomania), the Great Work is now truly odd. It proposes satisfactions that are immense, solemn, and restricting. It insists that art must be true, not just interesting; a necessity, not just an experiment. It dwarfs other work, challenges the facile eclecticism of contemporary taste. It throws the admirer into a state of crisis.

Syberberg assumes importance both for his art (*the* art of the twentieth century: film) and for his subject (*the* subject of the twentieth century: Hitler). The assumptions are familiar, crude, plausible. But they hardly prepare us for the scale and virtuosity with which he conjures up the ultimate subjects: hell, paradise lost, the apocalypse, the last days of mankind. Leavening romantic grandiosity with modernist ironies, Syberberg offers a spectacle about spectacle: evoking "the big show" called history in a variety of dramatic modes—fairy tale, circus, morality play, allegorical pageant, magic ceremony, philosophical dialogue, *Totentanz*—with an imaginary cast of tens of millions and, as protagonist, the Devil himself.

The Romantic notions of the maximal so congenial to Syberberg such as the boundless talent, the ultimate subject, and the most inclusive art—these notions confer an excruciating sense of possibility. Syberberg's confidence that his art is adequate to his great subject derives from his idea of cinema as a way of knowing that incites speculation to take a self-reflexive turn. Hitler is depicted through examining our relation to Hitler (the theme is "our Hitler" and "Hitler-in-us"), as the rightly unassimilable horrors of the Nazi era are represented in Syberberg's film as images or signs. (Its title isn't *Hitler* but, precisely, *Hitler, a Film . . .*)

To simulate atrocity convincingly is to risk making the audience passive, reinforcing witless stereotypes, confirming distance and creating fascination. Convinced that there is a morally (and aesthetically) correct way for a filmmaker to confront Nazism, Syberberg can make no use of any of the stylistic conventions of fiction that pass for realism. Neither can he rely on documents to show how it "really" was. Like its simulation as fiction, the display of atrocity in the form of photographic evidence risks being tacitly pornographic. Further, the truths it conveys, unmediated, about the past are slight. Film clips of the Nazi period cannot speak for themselves; they require a voice—explaining, commenting, interpreting. But the relation of the voice-over to a film document, like that of the caption to a still photograph, is merely adhesive. In contrast to the pseudo-objective style of narration in most documentaries, the two ruminating voices which suffuse Syberberg's film constantly express pain, grief, dismay.

Rather than devise a spectacle in the past tense, either by attempting to simulate "unrepeatable reality" (Syberberg's phrase) or by showing it in photographic document, he proposes a spectacle in the present tense—"adventures in the head." Of course, for such a devoutly anti-realist aesthetician historical reality is, by definition, unrepeatable. Reality can only be grasped indirectly—seen reflected in a mirror, staged in the theater of the mind. Syberberg's synoptic drama is radically subjective, without being solipsistic. It is a ghostly film—haunted by his great cinematic models (Méliès, Eisenstein) and anti-models (Riefenstahl, Hollywood); by German Romanticism; and, above all, by the music of Wagner and the case of Wagner. A posthumous film, in the era of cinema's unprecedented mediocrity—full of cinéphile myths, about cinema as the ideal space of the imagination and cinema history as an exemplary history of the twentieth century (the martyrdom of Eisenstein by Stalin, the excommunication of von Stroheim by Hollywood); and of cinéphile hyperboles: he designates Riefenstahl's *Triumph of the Will* as Hitler's "only lasting monument, apart from the newsreels of his war." One of the film's conceits is that Hitler, who never visited the front and watched the war every night through newsreels, was a kind of moviemaker. Germany, a Film by Hitler.

Syberberg has cast his film as a phantasmagoria: the meditative-sensuous form favored by Wagner which distends time and results in works that the unpassionate find overlong. Its length is suitably exhaustive—seven hours;

and, like the *Ring*, it is a tetralogy. The titles of its four parts are: *Hitler, a Film from Germany*; *A German Dream*; *The End of a Winter's Tale*; *We, Children of Hell*. A film, a dream, a tale. Hell.

In contrast to the lavish de Mille-like décors that Wagner projected for his tetralogy, Syberberg's film is a cheap fantasy. The large sound studio in Munich where the film was shot in 1977 (in twenty days—after four years of preparation) is furnished as a surreal landscape. The wide shot of the set at the beginning of the film displays many of the modest props that will recur in different sequences, and suggests the multiple uses Syberberg will make of this space: as a space of rumination (the wicker chair, the plain table, the candelabra); a space of theatrical assertion (the canvas director's chair, the giant black megaphone, the upturned masks); a space of emblems (models of the polyhedron in Dürer's *Melencolia I*, and of the ash tree from the set of the first production of *Die Walküre*); a space of moral judgment (a large globe, a life-size rubber sex-doll); a space of melancholy (the dead leaves strewn on the floor).

This allegory-littered wasteland (as limbo, as the moon) is designed to hold multitudes, in their contemporary, that is posthumous, form. It is really the land of the dead, a cinematic Valhalla. Since all the characters of the Nazi catastrophe-melodrama are dead, what we see are their ghosts—as puppets, as spirits, as caricatures of themselves. Carnivalesque skits alternate with arias and soliloquies, narratives, reveries. The two ruminating presences (André Heller, Harry Baer) keep up, on screen and off, an endless intellectual melody—lists, judgments, questions, historical anecdotes, as well as multiple characterizations of the film and the consciousness behind it.

The muse of Syberberg's historic epic is cinema itself ("the world of our inner projections"), represented on the wasteland set by Black Maria, the tarpaper shack built for Thomas Edison in 1893 as the first film studio. By invoking cinema as Black Maria, that is, recalling the artisanal simplicity of its origins, Syberberg also points to his own achievement. Using a small crew, with time for only one take of many long and complex shots, this technically ingenious inventor of fantasy managed to film virtually all of what he intended as he had envisaged it; and all of it is on the screen. (Perhaps only a spectacle as underbudgeted as this one—it cost $500,000—can remain wholly responsive to the intentions and improvisations of a single creator.) Out of this ascetic way of filmmaking, with its codes of deliberate naïveté, Syberberg has made a film that is both stripped-down and lush, discursive and spectacular.

Syberberg provides spectacle out of his modest means by replicating and reusing the key elements as many times as possible. Having each actor play several roles, the convention inspired by Brecht, is an aspect of this aesthetics of multiple use. Many things appear at least twice in the film, once full-sized and once miniaturized—for example, a thing and its photograph; and all the Nazi notables appear played by actors and as puppets. Edison's Black Maria, the primal film studio, is presented in four ways: as a large structure, indeed the principal item of the master set, from which actors appear and into which they disappear; as toy structures in two sizes, the tinier on a snowy landscape inside a glass globe, which can be held in an actor's hand, shaken, ruminated upon; and in a photographic blowup of the globe.

Syberberg uses multiple approaches, multiple voices.

/ 142

The libretto is a medley of imaginary discourse and the *ipsissima verba* of Hitler, Himmler, Goebbels, Speer, and such backstage characters as Himmler's Finnish masseur Felix Kersten and Hitler's valet Karl-Wilhelm Krause. The complex sound track often provides two texts at once. Interspersed between and intermittently overlaid on the speeches of actors—a kind of auditory back-projection— are historical sound documents, such as snatches from speeches by Hitler and Goebbels, from wartime news broadcasts by German radio and the BBC. The stream of words also includes cultural references in the form of quotations (often left unattributed), such as Einstein on war and peace, a passage from Marinetti's Futurist Manifesto—and the whole verbal polyphony swelled by excerpts from the pantheon of German music, mostly Wagner. A passage from, say, *Tristan und Isolde* or the chorus of Beethoven's Ninth is used as another kind of historical quotation which complements or comments on what is being said, simultaneously, by an actor.

On the screen, a varying stock of emblematic props and images supplies more associations. Doré engravings for the *Inferno* and the Bible, Graff's portrait of Frederick the Great, the signature still from Méliès's *A Trip to the Moon*, Runge's *Morning*, Caspar David Friedrich's *The Frozen Ocean* are among the visual references that appear (by a canny technique of slide projection) behind the actors. The image is constructed on the same assemblage principle as the sound track except that, while we hear many historical sound documents, Syberberg makes sparing use of visual documents from the Nazi era.

Méliès in the foreground, Lumière very much in the background. Syberberg's meta-spectacle virtually swallows up the photographic document: when we see the Nazi reality on film, it is as film. Behind a seated, ruminating actor (Heller) appears some private 8 and 16 mm. footage of Hitler—indistinct, rather unreal. Such bits of film are not used to show how anything "really" was: film clips, slides of paintings, movie stills all have the same status. Actors play in front of photographic blowups that show legendary places without people: these empty, almost abstract, oddly scaled views of Ludwig II's Venus Grotto at Linderhof, Wagner's villa in Bayreuth, the conference room in the Reich Chancellery in Berlin, the terrace of Hitler's villa in Berchtesgaden, the ovens at Auschwitz are a more stylized kind of allusion. They are also a ghostly décor rather than a "real" set, with which Syberberg can play illusionist tricks reminiscent of Méliès: having the actor appear to be walking within a deep-focus photograph, ending a scene with the actor turning and vanishing into a backdrop that had appeared to be seamless.

Nazism is known by allusion, through fantasy, in quotation. Quotations are both literal, like an Auschwitz's survivor's testimony, and, more commonly, fanciful cross-references—as when the hysterical SS man recites the child murderer's plea from Lang's *M*; or Hitler, in a tirade of self-exculpation, rising in a cobwebby toga from the grave of Richard Wagner, quotes Shylock's "If you prick us, do we not bleed?" Like the photographic images and the props, the actors are also stand-ins for the real. Most speech is monologue or monodrama, whether by a single actor talking directly to the camera, that is, the audience, or by actors half talking to themselves (as in the scene of Himmler and his masseur) or declaiming in a row (the rotting puppets in hell). As in a Surrealist tableau, the presence of the inanimate makes its ironic comment on the supposedly alive. Actors talk to, or on behalf of, puppets of Hitler, Goebbels, Goering, Himmler, Eva Braun, Speer. Several scenes set actors among department-store mannequins, or among the life-size photographic cutouts of legendary ghouls from the German silent cinema (Mabuse, Alraune, Caligari, Nosferatu) and of the archetypal Germans photographed by August Sander. Hitler is a recurrent multiform presence, depicted in memory, through burlesque, in historical travesty.

Quotations in the film; the film as a mosaic of stylistic quotations. To present Hitler in multiple guises and from many perspectives, Syberberg draws on disparate stylistic sources: Wagner, Méliès, Brechtian distancing techniques, homosexual baroque, puppet theater. This eclecticism is the mark of an extremely self-conscious, erudite, avid artist, whose choice of stylistic materials (blending high art and kitsch) is not as arbitrary as it might seem. Syberberg's film is, precisely, Surrealist in its eclecticism. Surrealism is a late variant of Romantic taste, a Romanticism that assumes a broken or posthumous world. It is Romantic taste with a leaning toward pastiche. Surrealist works proceed by conventions of dismemberment and reaggregation, in the spirit of pathos and irony; these conventions include the inventory (or open-ended list); the technique of duplication by miniaturization; the hyper-development of the art of quotation. By means of these conventions, particularly the circulation and recycling of visual and aural quotations, Syberberg's film simultaneously inhabits many places, many times—his principal device of dramatic and visual irony.

His broadest irony is to mock all this complexity by presenting his meditation on Hitler as something simple: a tale told in the presence of a child. His nine-year-old daughter is the mute somnambulistic witness, crowned by loops of celluloid, who wanders through the steam-filled landscape of hell; who begins and closes each of the film's four parts. Alice in Wonderland, the spirit of cinema—she is surely meant as these. And Syberberg also evokes the symbolism of melancholy, identifying the child with Dürer's *Melencolia*: at the film's end she is posed inside a plump tear, gazing in front of the stars. Whatever the attributions, the image owes much to Surrealist taste. The condition of the somnambulist is a convention of Surrealist narrative. The person who moves through a Surrealist landscape is typically in a dreamy, becalmed state. The enterprise that takes one through a Surrealist landscape is always quixotic—hopeless, obsessional; and, finally, self-regarding. An emblematic image in the film, one much admired by the Surrealists, is Ledoux's "Eye Reflecting the Interior of the Theater of Besançon" (1804). Ledoux's eye first appears on the set as a two-dimensional picture. Later it is a three-dimensional construction, an eye-as-theater in which one of the narrators (Baer) sees, projected at the rear, himself—in an earlier film by Syberberg, *Ludwig, Requiem for a Virgin King*, in which he played the lead. As Ledoux locates his theater in the eye, Syberberg locates his cinema inside the mind, where all associations are possible.

Syberberg's repertory of theatrical devices and images seems inconceivable without the freedoms and ironies introduced by Surrealist taste, and reflects many of its distinctive affections. Grand Guignol, puppet theater, the circus, and the films of Méliès were Surrealist passions. The taste for naïve theater and primitive cinema as well as for objects which miniaturize reality, for the art of Northern Romanticism (Dürer, Blake, Friedrich, Runge), for architecture as utopian fantasy (Ledoux) and as private delirium (Ludwig II)—the sensibility that encompasses all these is Surrealism. But there is an aspect of Surrealist taste that is alien to Syberberg—the surrender to chance, to the arbitrary; the fascination with the opaque, the meaningless, the mute. There is nothing arbitrary or aleatoric about his décor, no throw-away images or objects without emotional weight; indeed, certain relics and images in Syberberg's film have the force of personal talismans. Everything means, everything speaks. One mute presence, Syberberg's child, only sets off the film's unrelenting verbosity and intensity. Everything in the film is presented as having been already consumed by a mind.

When history takes place inside the head, public and private mythologies gain equal status. Unlike the other mega-films with whose epic ambitions it might be compared—*Intolerance, Napoleon, Ivan the Terrible I & II, 2001*—Syberberg's film is open to personal references as well as public ones. Public myths of evil are framed by the private mythologies of innocence, developed in two earlier films, *Ludwig* (1972, two hours twenty minutes) and *Karl May—In Search of Paradise Lost* (1974, three hours), which Syberberg treats as the first two parts of a trilogy on Germany that concludes with *Hitler, a Film from Germany*. Wagner's patron and victim, Ludwig II, is a recurrent figure of innocence. One of Syberberg's talismanic images—it ends *Ludwig* and is reused in *Hitler, a Film . . .* —shows Ludwig as a bearded, weeping child. The image that opens the Hitler film is of Ludwig's Winter Garden in Munich—a paradisiacal landscape of Alps, palm trees, lake, tent, gondola, which figures throughout *Ludwig*.

Each of the three films stands on its own, but so far as they are regarded as comprising a trilogy, it is worth noting that *Ludwig* feeds more images to *Hitler, a Film from Germany* than does the second film, *Karl May*. Parts of *Karl May*, with its "real" sets and actors, come closer to linear, mimetic dramaturgy than anything in *Ludwig* or in the incomparably more ambitious and profound film on Hitler. But, like all artists with a taste for pastiche, Syberberg has only a limited feeling for what is understood as realism. The pasticheur's style is essentially a style of fantasy.

Syberberg has devised a particularly German variety of spectacle: the moralized horror show. In the excruciating banalities of the valet's narrative, in a burlesque of Chaplin's impersonation of Hitler in *The Great Dictator*, in a Grand Guignol skit about Hitler's sperm—the Devil is a familiar spirit. Hitler is even allowed to share in the pathos of miniaturization: the Hitler-puppet (dressed, undressed, reasoned with) held on a ventriloquist's knees, the cloth dog with the Hitler face, carried mournfully by the child. The spectacle assumes familiarity with the incidents and personages of German history and culture, the Nazi regime, World War II; alludes freely to events in the three decades since Hitler's death. While the present is reduced to being the legacy of the past, the past is embellished with knowledge of its future. In *Ludwig*, this open-ended historical itinerary seems like cool (Brechtian?) irony—as when Ludwig I cites Brecht. In *Hitler, a Film from Germany* the irony of anachronism is weightier. Syberberg denies that the events of Nazism were part of the ordinary gait and demeanor of history. ("They said it was the end of the world," muses one of the puppet-masters. "And it

was.") His film takes Nazism at its (Hitler's, Goebbels')
word, as a venture in apocalypse, as a cosmology of a New
Ice Age, in other words as an eschatology of evil; and itself
takes place at a kind of end-of-time, a Messianic time (to
use Benjamin's term) which imposes the duty of trying to
do justice to the dead. Hence, the long solemn roll call of
the accomplices of Nazism ("Those whom we must not
forget"), then of some exemplary victims—one of the several points at which the film seems to end.

Syberberg has cast his film in the first person: as the
action of one artist assuming the German duty to confront
fully the horror of Nazism. Like many German intellectuals of the past, Syberberg treats his Germanness as a
moral vocation and regards Germany as the cockpit of
European conflicts. ("The twentieth century . . . a film
from Germany," says one of the ruminators.) Syberberg
was born in 1935 in what was to become East Germany and
left in 1953 for West Germany, where he has lived ever
since; but the true provenance of his film is the extrater-
ritorial Germany of the spirit whose first great citizen was
that self-styled *romantique défroqué* Heine, and whose last
great citizen was Thomas Mann. "To be the spiritual
battlefield of European antagonisms—that's what it means
to be German," Mann declared in his *Reflections of an
Unpolitical Man*, written during World War I, sentiments
that had not changed when he wrote *Doctor Faustus* as an
old man in exile in the late 1940s. Syberberg's view of
Nazism as the explosion of the German demonic recalls
Mann, as does his unfashionable insistence on Germany's
collective guilt (the theme of "Hitler-in-us"). The narrators' repeated challenge, "Who would Hitler be without
us?," also echoes Mann, who wrote an essay in 1939 called

"Brother Hitler" in which he argues that "the whole thing is a distorted phase of Wagnerism." Like Mann, Syberberg regards Nazism as the grotesque fulfillment—and betrayal —of German Romanticism. It may seem odd that Syberberg, who was a child during the Nazi era, shares so many themes with someone so ancien-régime. But there is much that is old-fashioned about Syberberg's sensibility (one consequence, perhaps, of being educated in a Communist country)—including the vividness with which he identifies with that Germany whose greatest citizens have gone into exile.

Although it draws on innumerable versions and impressions of Hitler, the film offers very few ideas about Hitler. For the most part they are the theses formulated in the ruins: the thesis that "Hitler's work" was "the eruption of the satanic principle in world history" (Meinecke's *The German Catastrophe*, written two years before *Doctor Faustus*); the thesis, expressed by Horkheimer in *The Eclipse of Reason*, that Auschwitz was the logical culmination of Western progress. Starting in the 1950s, when the ruins of Europe were rebuilt, more complex theses—political, sociological, economic—prevailed about Nazism. (Horkheimer eventually repudiated his argument of 1946.) In reviving those unmodulated views of thirty years ago, their indignation, their pessimism, Syberberg's film makes a strong case for their moral appropriateness.

Syberberg proposes that we really listen to what Hitler said—to the kind of cultural revolution Nazism was, or claimed to be; to the spiritual catastrophe it was, and still is. By Hitler Syberberg does not mean only the real historical monster, responsible for the deaths of tens of millions. He evokes a kind of Hitler-substance that outlives Hitler, a phantom presence in modern culture, a protean principle of evil that saturates the present and remakes the past. Syberberg's film alludes to familiar genealogies, real and symbolic: from Romanticism to Hitler, from Wagner to Hitler, from Caligari to Hitler, from kitsch to Hitler. And, in the hyperbole of woe, he insists on some new filiations: from Hitler to pornography, from Hitler to the soul-less consumer society of the Federal Republic, from Hitler to the rude coercions of the DDR. In using Hitler thus, there is some truth, some unconvincing attributions. It is true that Hitler has contaminated Romanticism and Wagner, that much of nineteenth-century German culture is, retroactively, haunted by Hitler. (As, say, nineteenth-century Russian culture is not haunted by Stalin.) But it is not true that Hitler engendered the modern, post-Hitlerian plastic consumer society. That was already well on the way when the Nazis took power. Indeed, it could be argued —contra Syberberg—that Hitler was in the long run an irrelevance, an attempt to halt the historical clock; and that communism is what ultimately mattered in Europe, not fascism. Syberberg is more plausible when he asserts that the DDR resembles the Nazi state, a view for which he has been denounced by the left in West Germany; like most intellectuals who grew up under a communist regime and moved to a bourgeois-democratic one, he is singularly free of left-wing pieties. It could also be argued that Syberberg has unduly simplified his moralist's task by the extent to which, like Mann, he identifies the inner history of Germany with the history of Romanticism.

Syberberg's notion of history as catastrophe recalls the long German tradition of regarding history eschatologically, as the history of the spirit. Comparable views today are more likely to be entertained in Eastern Europe than in Germany. Syberberg has the moral intransigence, the lack of respect for literal history, the heartbreaking seriousness of the great illiberal artists from the Russian empire—with their fierce convictions about the primacy of spiritual over material (economic, political) causation, the irrelevance of the categories "left" and "right," the existence of absolute evil. Appalled by the extensiveness of German support for Hitler, Syberberg calls the Germans "a Satanic people."

The devil story that Mann devised to sum up the Nazi demonic was narrated by someone who does not understand. Thereby Mann suggested that evil so absolute may be, finally, beyond comprehension or the grasp of art. But the obtuseness of the narrator of *Doctor Faustus* is too much insisted on. Mann's irony backfires: Serenus Zeitblom's fatuous modesty of understanding seems like Mann's confession of inadequacy, his inability to give full voice to grief. Syberberg's film about the devil, though sheathed in ironies, affirms our ability to understand and our obligation to grieve. Dedicated, as it were, to grief, the film begins and ends with Heine's lacerating words: "I think of Germany in the night and sleep leaves me, I can no longer close my eyes, I weep hot tears." Grief is the burden of the calm, rueful, musical soliloquies of Baer and Heller; neither reciting nor declaiming, they are simply speaking out, and listening to these grave, intelligent voices seething with grief is itself a civilizing experience.

The film carries without any condescension a vast legacy of information about the Nazi period. But information is assumed. The film is not designed to meet a standard of information but claims to address a (hypothetical) therapeutic ideal. Syberberg repeatedly says that his film is addressed to the German "inability to mourn," that it undertakes "the work of mourning" (*Trauerarbeit*). These phrases recall the famous essay Freud wrote deep in World War I, "Mourning and Melancholia," which connects melancholy with the inability to work through grief; and the application of this formula in an influential psychoanalytic study of postwar Germany by Alexander and Margarete Mitscherlich, *The Inability to Mourn*, published in Germany in 1967, which diagnoses the Germans as afflicted by mass melancholia, the result of the continuing denial of their collective responsibility for the Nazi past and their persistent refusal to mourn. Syberberg has appropriated the well-known Mitscherlich thesis (without ever mentioning their book), but one might doubt that his film was inspired by it. It seems more likely that Syberberg found in the notion of *Trauerarbeit* a psychological and moral justification for his aesthetics of repetition and recycling. It takes time—and much hyperbole—to work through grief.

So far as the film can be considered as an act of mourning, what is interesting is that it is conducted in the style of mourning—by exaggeration, repetition. It provides an overflow of information: the method of saturation. Syberberg is an artist of excess: thought is a kind of excess, the surplus production of ruminations, images, associations, emotions connected with, evoked by, Hitler. Hence the film's length, its circular arguments, its several beginnings, its four or five endings, its many titles, its plurality of styles, its vertiginous shifts of perspective on Hitler, from below or beyond. The most wonderful shift occurs in Part II, when the valet's forty-minute monologue with its mesmerizing trivia about Hitler's taste in underwear and shaving cream and breakfast food is followed by Heller's musings on the unreality of the idea of the galaxies. (It is the verbal equivalent of the cut in *2001* from the bone thrown in the air by a primate to the space ship—surely the most spectacular cut in the history of cinema.) Syberberg's idea is to exhaust, to empty his subject.

Syberberg measures his ambitions by the standards of Wagner, although living up to the legendary attributes of a German genius is no easy task in the consumer society of the Federal Republic. He considers that *Hitler, a Film from Germany* is not just a film, as Wagner did not want the *Ring* and *Parsifal* to be considered operas or to be part of the normal repertory of opera houses. Its defiant, seductive length, which prevents the film from being distributed conventionally, is very Wagnerian, as is Syberberg's reluctance (until recently) to let it be shown except in special circumstances, encouraging seriousness. Also Wagnerian are Syberberg's ideal of exhaustiveness and profundity; his sense of mission; his belief in art as a radical act; his taste for scandal; his polemical energies (he is incapable of writing an essay that is not a manifesto); his taste for the grandiose. Grandiosity is, precisely, Syberberg's great subject. The protagonists of his trilogy about Germany—Ludwig II, Karl May, Hitler—are all megalomaniacs, liars, reckless dreamers, virtuosi of the grandiose. (Very different sorts of documentaries Syberberg made for German television between 1967 and 1975 also express his fascination with the self-assured and self-obsessed: *Die Grafen Pocci*, about an aristocratic German family; portraits of German film stars; and the five-hour interview-

/154

film on Wagner's daughter-in-law and Hitler's friend, *The Confessions of Winifred Wagner.*)

Syberberg is a great Wagnerian, the greatest since Thomas Mann, but his attitude to Wagner and the treasures of German Romanticism is not only pious. It contains more than a bit of malice, the touch of the cultural vandal. To evoke the grandeur and the failure of Wagnerianism, *Hitler, a Film from Germany* uses, recycles, parodies elements of Wagner. Syberberg means his film to be an anti-*Parsifal*, and hostility to Wagner is one of its leitmotifs: the spiritual filiation of Wagner and Hitler. The whole film could be considered a profaning of Wagner, undertaken with a full sense of the gesture's ambiguity, for Syberberg is attempting to be both inside and outside his own deepest sources as an artist. (The graves of Wagner and Cosima behind Villa Wahnfried recur as an image; and one scene satirizes that most ineffectual of profanations, when black American GIs jitterbugged on the graves after the war.) For it is from Wagner that Syberberg's film gets its biggest boost—its immediate intrinsic claim on the sublime. As the film opens, we hear the beginning of the prelude to *Parsifal* and see the word GRAIL in fractured blocky letters. Syberberg claims that his aesthetic is Wagnerian, that is, musical. But it might be more correct to say that his film is in a mimetic relation to Wagner, and in part a parasitic one—as *Ulysses* is in a parasitic relation to the history of English literature.

Syberberg takes very literally, more literally than Eisenstein ever did, the promise of film as a synthesis of the plastic arts, music, literature, and theater—the modern fulfillment of Wagner's idea of the total work of art. (It has often been said that Wagner, had he lived in the twentieth century, would have been a filmmaker.) But the modern *Gesamtkunstwerk* tends to be an aggregation of seemingly disparate elements instead of a synthesis. For Syberberg there is always something more, and different, to say—as the two films on Ludwig he made in 1972 attest. *Ludwig, Requiem for a Virgin King*, which became the first film in his trilogy about Germany, pays delirious homage to the ironic theatricality and overripe pathos of such filmmakers as Cocteau, Carmelo Bene, and Werner Schroeter. *Theodor Hirneis*, the other film, is an austere Brechtian monodrama of ninety minutes with Ludwig's cook as its one character—it anticipates the valet's narrative in *Hitler, a Film from Germany*—and was inspired by Brecht's unfinished novel on the life of Julius Caesar narrated by his slave. Syberberg considers that he began as a disciple of Brecht, and in 1952 and 1953 filmed several of Brecht's productions in East Berlin.

According to Syberberg, his work comes from "the duality Brecht/Wagner"; that is the "aesthetic scandal" he claims to have "sought." In interviews he invariably cites both as his artistic fathers, partly (it may be supposed) to neutralize the politics of one by the politics of the other and place himself beyond issues of left and right; partly to appear more evenhanded than he is. But he is inevitably more of a Wagnerian than a Brechtian, because of the way the inclusive Wagnerian aesthetic accommodates contraries of feeling (including ethical feeling and political bias). Baudelaire heard in Wagner's music "the ultimate scream of a soul driven to its utmost limits," while Nietzsche, even after giving up on Wagner, still praised him as a great "miniaturist" and "our greatest melancholiac in music"—and both were right. Wagner's contraries reappear in Syberberg: the radical democrat and the right-wing elitist, the aesthete and the moralist, rant and rue.

Syberberg's polemical genealogy, Brecht/Wagner, obscures other influences on the film; in particular, what he owes to Surrealist ironies and images. But even the role of Wagner seems a more complex affair than Syberberg's enthrallment with the art and life of Wagner would indicate. Apart from the Wagner that Syberberg has appropriated, one is tempted to say expropriated, this Wagnerianism is, properly, an attenuated affair—a fascinatingly belated example of the art which grew out of the Wagnerian aesthetic: Symbolism. (Both Symbolism and Surrealism could be considered as late developments of the Romantic sensibility.) Symbolism was the Wagnerian aesthetic turned into a procedure of creation for all the arts; further subjectivized, pulled toward abstraction. What Wagner wanted was an ideal theater, a theater of maximal emotions purged of distractions and irrelevancies. Thus Wagner chose to conceal the orchestra of the Bayreuth Festspielhaus under a black wooden shell, and once quipped that, having invented the invisible orchestra, he wished he could invent the invisible stage. The Symbolists found the invisible stage. Events were to be withdrawn from reality, so to speak, and restaged in the ideal theater of the mind.* And Wagner's fantasy of the invisible stage was fulfilled more literally in that immaterial stage, cinema.

---

* "Instead of trying to produce the largest possible reality outside himself," Jacques Rivière has written, the Symbolist artist "tries to consume as much as possible within himself. . . . he offers his mind as a kind of ideal theater where [events] can be acted out without becoming visible." Rivière's essay on Symbolism, "Le Roman d'Aventure" (1913), is the best account of it I know.

Syberberg's film is a magistral rendering of the Symbolist potentialities of cinema and probably the most ambitious Symbolist work of this century. He construes cinema as a kind of ideal mental activity, being both sensuous and reflective, which takes up where reality leaves off: cinema not as the fabrication of reality but as "a continuation of reality by other means." In Syberberg's meditation on history in a sound studio, events are visualized (with the aid of Surrealist conventions) while remaining in a deeper sense invisible (the Symbolist ideal). But because it lacks the stylistic homogeneity that was typical of Symbolist works, *Hitler, a Film from Germany* has a vigor that Symbolists would forgo as vulgar. Its impurities rescue the film from what was most rarefied about Symbolism without making its reach any less indeterminate and comprehensive.

The Symbolist artist is above all a mind, a creator-mind that (distilling the Wagnerian grandiosity and intensity) sees everything, that is able to permeate its subject; and eclipses it. Syberberg's meditation on Hitler has the customary overbearingness of this mind, and the characteristic porousness of the overextended Symbolist mental structures: soft-edge arguments that begin "I think of . . . ," verbless sentences that evoke rather than explain. Conclusions are everywhere but nothing concludes. All the parts of a Symbolist narrative are simultaneous; that is, all coexist simultaneously in this superior, overbearing mind.

The function of this mind is not to tell a story (at the start the story is behind it, as Rivière pointed out) but to confer meaning in unlimited amounts. Actions, figures, individual bias of décor can have, ideally do have, multiple

meanings—for example, the charge of meanings Syberberg attaches to the figure of the child. He appears to be
seeking, from a more subjective standpoint, what Eisenstein
prescribes with his theory of "overtonal montage." (Eisenstein, who saw himself in the tradition of Wagner and the
Gesamtkunstwerk and in his writings quotes copiously
from the French Symbolists, was the greatest exponent of
Symbolist aesthetics in cinema.) The film overflows with
meanings of varying accessibility, and there are further
meanings from relics and talismans on the set which the
audience can't possibly know about.* The Symbolist artist
is not primarily interested in exposition, explanation,
communication. It seems fitting that Syberberg's dramaturgy consists in talk addressed to those who cannot talk
back: to the dead (one can put words in their mouths) and
to one's own daughter (who has no lines). The Symbolist
narrative is always a posthumous affair; its subject is precisely something that is assumed. Hence, Symbolist art is
characteristically dense, difficult. Syberberg is appealing
(intermittently) to another process of knowing, as is indi-
cated by one of the film's principal emblems, Ledoux's
ideal theater in the form of an eye—the Masonic eye; the
eye of intelligence, of esoteric knowledge. But Syberberg

---

* For example, on Baer's table Syberberg put a piece of wood from
Ludwig's Hundinghütte, the playhouse at Linderhof (it burned down
in 1945) inspired by the designs for Act I of *Die Walküre* in the first
two productions; elsewhere on the set are a stone from Bayreuth,
a relic from Hitler's villa at Berchtesgaden, and other treasures. In
one instance, talismans were furnished by the actor: Syberberg asked
Heller to bring some objects that were precious to him, and Heller's
photograph of Joseph Roth and a small Buddha can just be made out
(if one knows they're there) on his table while he delivers the cosmos
monologue at the end of Part II and the long monologue of Part IV.

wants, passionately wants his film to be understood; and in some parts it is as overexplicit as in other parts it is encoded.

The Symbolist relation of a mind to its subject is consummated when the subject is vanquished, undone, used up. Thus Syberberg's grandest conceit is that with his film he may have "defeated" Hitler—exorcised him. This splendidly outrageous hyperbole caps Syberberg's profound understanding of Hitler as an image. (If from *The Cabinet of Dr. Caligari* to Hitler, then why not from Hitler to *Hitler, a Film from Germany*? The end.) It also follows from Syberberg's Romantic views of the sovereignty of the imagination, and his flirtation with esoteric ideas of knowing, with notions of art as magic or spiritual alchemy, and of the imagination as a purveyor of the powers of blackness.

Heller's monologue in Part IV leads toward a roll call of myths that can be regarded as metaphors for the esoteric powers of cinema—starting with Edison's Black Maria ("the black studio of our imagination"); evoking black stones (of the Kaaba; of Dürer's *Melencolia*, the presiding image of the film's complex iconography); and ending with a modern image: cinema as the imagination's black hole. Like a black hole, or our fantasy about it, cinema collapses space and time. The image perfectly describes the excruciating fluency of Syberberg's film: its insistence on occupying different spaces and times simultaneously. It seems apt that Syberberg's private mythology of subjective cinema concludes with an image drawn from science fiction. A subjective cinema of these ambitions and moral energy logically mutates into science fiction. Thus Syberberg's film begins with the stars and ends, like *2001*, with the stars and a star-child.

Evoking Hitler by means of myth and travesty, fairy tales and science fictions, Syberberg conducts his own rites of deconsecration: the Grail has been destroyed (Syberberg's anti-*Parsifal* opens and closes with the word GRAIL —the film's true title); it is no longer permissible to dream of redemption. Syberberg defends his mythologizing of history as a skeptic's enterprise: myth as "the mother of irony and pathos," not myths which stimulate new systems of belief. But someone who believes that Hitler was Germany's "fate" is hardly a skeptic. Syberberg is the sort of artist who wants to have it both—all—ways. The method of his film is contradiction, irony. And, exercising his ingenious talent for naïveté, he also claims to transcend this complexity. He relishes notions of innocence and pathos —the traditions of Romantic idealism; some nonsense around the figure of a child (his daughter, the infant in Runge's *Morning*, Ludwig as a bearded, weeping child); dreams of an ideal world purified of its complexity and mediocrity.

The earlier parts of Syberberg's trilogy are elegiac portraits of last-ditch dreamers of paradise: Ludwig II, who built castles which were stage sets and paid for Wagner's dream factory at Bayreuth; Karl May, who romanticized American Indians, Arabs, and other exotics in his immensely popular novels, the most famous of which, *Winnetou*, chronicles the destruction of beauty and bravery by the coming of modern technological civilization. Ludwig and Karl May attract Syberberg as gallant, doomed practitioners of the Great Refusal, the refusal of modern industrial civilization. What Syberberg loathes most, such as pornography and the commercialization of culture, he identifies with the modern. (In this stance of utter superiority to the modern, Syberberg recalls the author of

Art and Crisis, Hans Sedlmayr, with whom he studied art history at the University of Munich in the fifties.) The film is a work of mourning for the modern and what precedes it, and opposes it. If Hitler is also a "utopian," as Syberberg calls him, then Syberberg is condemned to be a post-utopian, a utopian who acknowledges that utopian feelings have been hopelessly defiled. Syberberg does not believe in a "new human being"—that perennial theme of cultural revolution on both the left and the right. For all his attraction to the credo of romantic genius, what he really believes in is Goethe and a thorough Gymnasium education.

Of course, one can find the usual contradictions in Syberberg's film—the poetry of utopia, the futility of utopia; rationalism and magic. And that only confirms what kind of film *Hitler, a Film from Germany* really is. Science fiction is precisely the genre which dramatizes the mix of nostalgia for utopia with dystopian fantasies and dread; the dual conviction that the world is ending and that it is on the verge of a new beginning. Syberberg's film about history is also a moral and cultural science fiction. Starship Goethe-Haus.

Syberberg manages to perpetuate in a melancholy, attenuated form something of Wagner's notions of art as therapy, as redemption, and as catharsis. He calls cinema "the most beautiful compensation" for the ravages of modern history, a kind of "redemption" to "our senses oppressed by progress." That art does in sorts redeem reality, by being better than reality—that is the ultimate Symbolist belief. Syberberg makes of cinema the last, most inclusive, most ghostly paradise. It is a view that reminds one of Godard. Syberberg's cinéphilia is another part of the immense pathos of his film; perhaps its only involuntary pathos. For whatever Syberberg says, cinema is now another lost paradise. In the era of cinema's unprecedented mediocrity, his masterpiece has something of the character of a posthumous event.

Spurning naturalism, the Romantics developed a melancholic style: intensely personal, the outreach of its tortured "I," centered on the agon of the artist and society. Mann gave the last profound expression to this romantic notion of the self's dilemma. Post-Romantics like Syberberg work in an impersonal melancholic style. What is central now is the relation between memory and the past: the clash between the possibility of remembering, of going on, and the lure of oblivion. Beckett gives one ahistorical version of this agon. Another version, obsessed with history, is Syberberg's.

To understand the past, and thereby to exorcise it, is Syberberg's largest moral ambition. His problem is that he cannot give anything up. So large is his subject—and everything Syberberg does makes it even larger—that he has to take many positions beyond it. One can find almost anything in Syberberg's passionately voluble film (short of a Marxist analysis or a shred of feminist awareness). Though he tries to be silent (the child, the stars), he can't stop talking; he's so immensely ardent, avid. As the film is ending, Syberberg wants to produce yet another ravishing image. Even when the film is finally over, he still wants to say more, and adds postscripts: the Heine epigraph, the citation of Mogadishu–Stammheim, a final oracular Syberberg-sentence, one last evocation of the Grail. The film is itself the creation of a world, from which (one feels) its creator has the greatest difficulty in extricating himself

—as does the admiring spectator; this exercise in the art of empathy produces a voluptuous anguish, an anxiety about concluding. Lost in the black hole of the imagination, the filmmaker has to make everything pass before him; identifies with each, and none.

Benjamin suggests that melancholy is the origin of true —that is, just—historical understanding. The true understanding of history, he said in the last text he wrote, is "a process of empathy whose origin is indolence of the heart, acedia." Syberberg shares something of Benjamin's positive, instrumental view of melancholy, and uses symbols of melancholy to punctuate his film. But Syberberg does not have the ambivalence, the slowness, the complexity, the tension of the Saturnian temperament. Syberberg is not a true melancholic but an *exalté*. But he uses the distinctive tools of the melancholic—the allegorical props, the talismans, the secret self-references; and with his irrepressible talent for indignation and enthusiasm, he is doing "the work of mourning." The word first appears at the end of the film he made on Winifred Wagner in 1975, where we read: "This film is part of Hans-Jürgen Syberberg's *Trauerarbeit*." What we see is Syberberg smiling.

Syberberg is a genuine elegaist. But his film is tonic. The poetic, husky-voiced, diffident logorrhea of Godard's late films discloses a morose conviction that speaking will never exorcise anything; in contrast to Godard's off-camera musings, the musings of Syberberg's personae (Heller and Baer) teem with calm assurance. Syberberg, whose temperament seems the opposite of Godard's, has a supreme confidence in language, in discourse, in eloquence itself. The film tries to say everything. Syberberg belongs to the race of creators like Wagner, Artaud, Céline, the late

Joyce, whose work annihilates other work. All are artists of endless speaking, endless melody—a voice that goes on and on. Beckett would belong to this race, too, were it not for some inhibitory force—sanity? elegance? good manners? less energy? deeper despair? So might Godard, were it not for the doubts he evidences about speaking, and the inhibition of feeling (both of sympathy and repulsion) that results from this sense of the impotence of speaking. Syberberg has managed to stay free of the standard doubts—doubts whose main function, now, seems to be to inhibit. The result is a film altogether exceptional in its emotional expressiveness, its great visual beauty, its sincerity, its moral passion, its concern with contemplative values.

The film tries to be everything. Syberberg's unprecedented ambition in *Hitler, a Film from Germany* is on another scale from anything one has seen on film. It is work that demands a special kind of attention and partisanship; and invites being reflected upon, reseen. The more one recognizes of its stylistic references and lore, the more the film vibrates. (Great art in the mode of pastiche invariably rewards study, as Joyce affirmed by daring to observe that the ideal reader of his work would be someone who could devote his life to it.) Syberberg's film belongs in the category of noble masterpieces which ask for fealty and can compel it. After seeing *Hitler, a Film from Germany*, there is Syberberg's film—and then there are the other films one admires. (Not too many these days, alas.) As was said ruefully of Wagner, he spoils our tolerance for the others.

(1979)

Remembering Barthes

Roland Barthes was sixty-four when he died last week, but the career was younger than that age suggests, for he was thirty-seven when he published his first book. After the tardy start there were many books, many subjects. One felt that he could generate ideas about anything. Put him in front of a cigar box and he would have one, two, many ideas—a little essay. It was not a question of knowledge (he couldn't have known much about some of the subjects he wrote about) but of alertness, a fastidious transcription of what *could* be thought about something, once it swam into the stream of attention. There was always some fine net of classification into which the phenomenon could be tipped.

In his youth he founded a university theater group, reviewed plays. And something of the theater, a profound love of appearances, colors his work when he began to exercise, at full strength, his vocation as a writer. His sense of ideas was dramaturgical: an idea was always in competition with another idea. Launching himself onto the inbred French intellectual stage, he took up arms against the traditional enemy: what Flaubert called "received ideas," and came to be known as the "bourgeois" mentality; what Marxists excoriated with the notion of false consciousness and Sartreians with bad faith; what Barthes, who had a degree in classics, was to label *doxa* (current opinion).

He started off in the postwar years, in the shadow of Sartre's moralistic questions, with manifestos about what literature is (*Writing Degree Zero*) and witty portraits of the idols of the bourgeois tribe (the articles collected in *Mythologies*). All his writings are polemical. But the deepest impulse of his temperament was not combative. It was celebratory. His debunking forays, which presumed the readiness to be made indignant by inanity, obtuseness, hypocrisy—these gradually subsided. He was more interested in bestowing praise, sharing his passions. He was a taxonomist of jubilation, and of the mind's earnest play.

What fascinated him were mental classifications. Hence, his outrageous book *Sade, Fourier, Loyola*, which, juxtaposing the three as intrepid champions of fantasy, obsessed classifiers of their own obsessions, obliterates all the issues of substance which make them *not* comparable. He was not a modernist in his tastes (despite his tendentious sponsorship of such avatars of literary modernism in Paris as Robbe-Grillet and Philippe Sollers), but he was a modernist in his practice. That is, he was irresponsible, playful, formalist—making literature in the act of talking about it. What stimulated him in a work was what it defended, and its systems of outrage. He was conscientiously interested in the perverse (he held the old-fashioned view that it was liberating).

Everything he wrote was interesting—vivacious, rapid, dense, *pointed*. Most of his books are collections of essays. (Among the exceptions is an early polemical book on Racine. A book of uncharacteristic length and explicitness on the semiology of fashion advertising, which he wrote to pay his academic dues, had the stuff of several virtuoso essays.) He produced nothing that could be called juvenilia; the elegant, exacting voice was there from the beginning. But the rhythm accelerated in the last decade, with a new book appearing every year or two. The thought had greater velocity. In his recent books, the essay form itself had splintered—perforating the essayist's reticence about the "I." The writing took on the freedoms and risks of the notebook. In *S/Z*, he reinvented a Balzac novella in the form of a doggedly ingenious textual gloss. There were the dazzling Borgesian appendices to *Sade, Fourier, Loyola*; the para-fictional pyrotechnics of the exchanges between text and photographs, between text and semi-obscured references in his autobiographical writings; the celebrations of illusion in his last book, on photography, published two months ago.

He was especially sensitive to the fascination exerted by that poignant notation, the photograph. Of the photographs he chose for *Roland Barthes by Roland Barthes*, perhaps the most moving shows an oversized child, Barthes at ten, being carried by, clinging to, his young mother (he titled it "asking for love"). He had an amorous relation to reality—and to writing, which for him were the same. He wrote about everything; besieged with requests to write occasional pieces, he accepted as many as he could; he wanted to be, and was often, seduced by a subject. (His subject became, more and more, seduction.) Like all writers, he complained of being overworked, of acceding to too many requests, of falling behind—but he was in fact one of the most disciplined, surest, most appetitive writers I've known. He found the time to give many eloquent, intellectually inventive interviews.

As a reader he was meticulous but not voracious. Almost everything he read he wrote about, so one could surmise that if he didn't write about it, he probably hadn't read it. He was as uncosmopolitan as most French intellectuals have been (an exception was his beloved Gide). He knew no foreign language well and had read little foreign literature, even in translation. The only foreign literature that seems to have touched him was German: Brecht was an early, potent enthusiasm; recently the sorrow discreetly recounted in *A Lover's Discourse* had led him to *The Sorrows of Young Werther* and to lieder. He was not curious enough to let his reading interfere with his writing.

He enjoyed being famous, with an ingenuous ever-renewed pleasure: in France one saw him often on television in recent years, and *A Lover's Discourse* was a best seller. And yet he spoke of how eerie it was to find his name every time he leafed through a magazine or newspaper. His sense of privacy was expressed exhibitionistically. Writing about himself, he often used the third person, as if he treated himself as a fiction. The later work contains much fastidious self-revelation, but always in a speculative form (no anecdote about the self which does not come bearing an idea between its teeth), and dainty meditation on the personal; the last article he published was about keeping a journal. All his work is an immensely complex enterprise of self-description.

Nothing escaped the attention of this devout, ingenious student of himself: the food, colors, odors he fancied; how he read. Studious readers, he once observed in a lecture in Paris, fall into two groups: those who underline their books and those who don't. He said that he belonged to the second group: he never made a mark in the book about which he planned to write but transcribed key excerpts onto cards. I have forgotten the theory he then confected about this preference, so I shall improvise my own. I connect his aversion to marking up books with the fact that he drew, and that this drawing, which he pursued seriously, was a kind of writing. The visual art that attracted him came from language, was indeed a variant of writing; he wrote essays on Erté's alphabet formed with human figures, on the calligraphic painting of Réquichot, of Twombly. His preference recalls that dead metaphor, a "body" of work—one does not usually write on a body one loves.

His temperamental dislike for the moralistic became more overt in recent years. After several decades' worth of dutiful adherence to right-minded (that is, left-wing) stands, the aesthete came out of the closet in 1974 when with some close friends and literary allies, Maoists of the moment, he went to China; in the scant three pages he wrote on his return, he said that he had been unimpressed by the moralizing and bored by the asexuality and the cultural uniformity. Barthes's work, along with that of Wilde and Valéry, gives being an aesthete a good name. Much of his recent writing is a celebration of the intelligence of the senses, and of the texts of sensation. Defending the

senses, he never betrayed the mind. Barthes did not entertain any Romantic clichés about the opposition between
sensual and mental alertness.

The work is about sadness overcome or denied. He had
decided that everything could be treated as a system—a
discourse, a set of classifications. Since everything was a
system, everything could be overcome. But eventually he
wearied of systems. His mind was too nimble, too ambitious, too drawn to risk. He seemed more anxious and vulnerable in recent years, as he became more productive than
ever. He had always, as he observed about himself,
"worked successively under the aegis of a great system
(Marx, Sartre, Brecht, semiology, the Text). Today it
seems to him that he writes more openly, more unprotect-
edly. . . ." He purged himself of the masters and master-
ideas from which he drew sustenance ("In order to speak
one must seek support from other texts," he explained),
only to stand in the shadow of himself. He became his own
Great Writer. He was in assiduous attendance at the sessions of a seven-day conference devoted to his work in 1977
—commenting, mildly interjecting, enjoying himself. He
published a review of his speculative book on himself
(Barthes on Barthes on Barthes). He became the shep-
herd of the flock of himself.

Vague torments, a feeling of insecurity, were ac-
knowledged—with the consoling implication that he was
on the edge of a great adventure. When he was in New
York a year and a half ago he avowed in public, with almost tremulous bravery, his intention to write a novel. Not
the novel one might expect from the critic who made
Robbe-Grillet seem for a while a central figure in contemporary letters; from the writer whose most wonderful

books—*Roland Barthes by Roland Barthes* and *A Lover's Discourse*—are themselves triumphs of modernist fiction in that tradition inaugurated by Rilke's *The Notebooks of Malte Laurids Brigge*, which crossbreeds fiction, essayistic speculation, and autobiography, in a linear-notebook rather than a linear-narrative form. No, not a modernist novel, but a "real" one, he said. Like Proust.

Privately he spoke of his longing to climb down from the academic summit—he'd held a chair at the Collège de France since 1977—in order to devote himself to this novel, and of his anxiety (on the face of it, unwarranted) about material security should he resign his teaching position. The death of his mother two years ago was a great blow. He recalled that it was only after Proust's mother died that Proust was able to begin *A la Recherche du temps perdu*. It was characteristic that he hoped to find a source of strength in his devastating grief.

As sometimes he wrote about himself in the third person he usually spoke of himself as without age, and alluded to his future as if he were a much younger man, which in a way he was. He yearned for greatness, yet felt himself to be (as he says in *Roland Barthes by Roland Barthes*) always in danger of "*recession* toward the minor thing, the old thing he is when 'left to himself.' " There was something reminiscent of Henry James about his temperament and the indefatigable subtlety of his mind. The dramaturgy of ideas yielded to the dramaturgy of feeling; his deepest interests were in things almost ineffable. His ambition had something of the Jamesian pathos, as did his self-doubts. If he could have written a great novel, one imagines it more like late James than like Proust.

It was hard to tell his age. Rather, he seemed to have no

age—appropriately, his life's chronology being askew. Though he spent much time with young people, he never affected anything of youth or its contemporary informalities. But he didn't seem to be old, though his movements were slow, his dress professorial. It was a body that knew how to rest: as García Marquez has observed, a writer must know how to rest. He was very industrious, yet also sybaritic. He had an intense but businesslike concern that he receive a regular ration of pleasure. He had been ill (tubercular) for many years when he was young, and one had the impression that he came into his body relatively late—as he did his mind, his productivity. He had sensual revelations abroad (Morocco, Japan); gradually, somewhat tardily he assumed the considerable sexual privileges that a man of his sexual tastes and great celebrity can command. There was something childlike about him, in the wistfulness, in the plump body and soft voice and beautiful skin, in the self-absorption. He liked to linger in cafés with students; he wanted to be taken to bars and discos—but, sexual transactions aside, his interest in you tended to be your interest in him. ("Ah, Susan. Toujours fidèle," were the words with which he greeted me, affectionately, when we last saw each other. I was, I am.)

He affirmed something childlike in his insistence, which he shared with Borges, that reading is a form of happiness, a form of joy. There was also something less than innocent about the claim, the hard edge of adult sexual clamorousness. With his boundless capacity for self-referring, he enrolled the invention of sense in the search for pleasure. The two were identified: reading as *jouissance* (the French word for joy that also means coming); the pleasure of the text. This too was typical. He was, as a voluptuary of the mind, a great reconciler. He had little feeling for the tragic. He was always finding the advantage of a disadvantage. Though he sounds many of the perennial themes of the modern culture critic, he was anything but catastrophe-minded. His work offers no visions of last judgments, civilization's doom, the inevitability of barbarism. It is not even elegiac. Old-fashioned in many of his tastes, he felt nostalgic for the decorum and the literacy of an older bourgeois order. But he found much that reconciled him to the modern.

He was extremely courteous, a bit unworldly, resilient— he detested violence. He had beautiful eyes, which are always sad eyes. There was something sad in all this talk about pleasure; *A Lover's Discourse* is a very sad book. But he had known ecstasy and wanted to celebrate it. He was a great lover of life (and denier of death); the purpose of his unwritten novel, he said, was to praise life, to express gratitude for being alive. In the serious business of pleasure, in the splendid play of his mind, there was always that undercurrent of pathos—now made more acute by his premature, mortifying death.

(1980)

Mind as Passion

> I cannot become modest; too many
> things burn in me; the old solu-
> tions are falling apart; nothing has
> been done yet with the new ones.
> So I begin, everywhere at once, as
> if I had a century ahead of me.
>
> —CANETTI, 1943

The speech that Elias Canetti delivered in Vienna on
the occasion of Hermann Broch's fiftieth birthday, in November 1936, intrepidly sets out some of Canetti's characteristic themes and is one of the handsomest tributes one
writer has ever paid to another. Such a tribute creates the
terms of a succession. When Canetti finds in Broch the
necessary attributes of a great writer—he is original; he
sums up his age; he opposes his age—he is delineating the
standards to which he has pledged himself. When he hails
Broch for reaching fifty (Canetti was then thirty-one) and
calls this just half of what a human life should be, he avows
that hatred of death and yearning for longevity that is the
signature of his work. When he extols Broch's intellectual
insatiability, evoking his vision of some unfettered state of
the mind, Canetti attests to equally fervent appetites of his

own. And by the magnanimity of his homage Canetti adds one more element to this portrait of the writer as his age's noble adversary: the writer as noble admirer.

His praise of Broch discloses much about the purity of moral position and intransigence Canetti aspires to, and his desire for strong, even overpowering models. Writing in 1965, Canetti evokes the paroxysms of admiration he felt for Karl Kraus in the twenties while a student in Vienna, in order to defend the value for a serious writer of being, at least for a while, in thrall to another's authority: the essay on Kraus is really about the ethics of admiration. He welcomes being challenged by worthy enemies (Canetti counts some "enemies"—Hobbes and Maistre— among his favorite writers); being strengthened by an unattainable, humbling standard. About Kafka, the most insistent of his admirations, he observes: "One turns good when reading him but without being proud of it."

So wholehearted is Canetti's relation to the duty and pleasure of admiring others, so fastidious is his sense of the writer's vocation, that humility—and pride—make him extremely self-involved in a characteristically impersonal way. He is preoccupied with being someone *he* can admire. This is a leading concern in *The Human Province*, Canetti's selection from the notebooks he kept between 1942 and 1972, during most of which time he was preparing and writing his great book *Crowds and Power* (1960). In these jottings Canetti is constantly prodding himself with the example of the great dead, identifying the intellectual necessity of what he undertakes, checking his mental temperature, shuddering with terror as the calendar sheds its leaves.

Other traits go with being a self-confident, generous admirer: fear of not being insolent or ambitious enough, impatience with the merely personal (one sign of a strong personality, as Canetti says, is the love of the impersonal), and aversion to self-pity. In the first volume of his autobiography, *The Tongue Set Free* (1977), what Canetti chooses to tell about his life features those whom he admired, whom he has learned from. Canetti relates with ardor how things worked for, not against, him; his is the story of a liberation: a mind—a language—a tongue "set free" to roam the world.

That world has a complex mental geography. Born in 1905 into a far-flung Sephardic family then quartered in Bulgaria (his father and his paternal grandparents came from Turkey), Canetti had a childhood rich in displacements. Vienna, where both his parents had gone to school, was the mental capital of all the other places, which included England, where his family moved when Canetti was six; Lausanne and Zurich, where he had some of his schooling; and sojourns in Berlin in the late twenties. It was to Vienna that his mother brought Canetti and his two younger brothers after his father died in Manchester in 1912, and from there that Canetti emigrated in 1938, spending a year in Paris and then moving to London, where he has lived ever since. Only in exile, he has noted, does one realize how much "the world has always been a world of exiles"—a characteristic observation, in that it deprives his plight of some of its particularity.

He has, almost by birthright, the exile writer's easily generalized relation to place: a place is a language. And knowing many languages is a way of claiming many places as one's territory. Family example (his paternal grandfather boasted of knowing seventeen languages), the local medley (in the Danube port city where he was born, Canetti says, one could hear seven or eight languages spoken every day), and the velocity of his childhood all facilitated an avid relation to language. To live was to acquire languages—his were Ladino, Bulgarian, German (the language his parents spoke to each other), English, French—and be "everywhere."

That German became the language of his mind confirms Canetti's placelessness. Pious tributes to Goethe's inspiration written in his notebook while the Luftwaffe's bombs fell on London ("If, despite everything, I should survive, then I owe it to Goethe") attest to that loyalty to German culture which would keep him always a foreigner in England—he has now spent well over half his life there—and which Canetti has the privilege and the burden of understanding, Jew that he is, as the higher cosmopolitanism. He will continue to write in German—"because I am Jewish," he noted in 1944. With this decision, not the one made by most Jewish intellectuals who were refugees from Hitler, Canetti chose to remain unsullied by hatred, a grateful son of German culture who wants to help make it what one can continue to admire. And he has.

Canetti is reputed to be the model for the philosopher figure in several of Iris Murdoch's early novels, such as Mischa Fox in *The Flight from the Enchanter* (dedicated to Canetti), a figure whose audacity and effortless superiority are an enigma to his intimidated friends.* Drawn from

---

* "What's odd about him?" he asked.

"Oh, I don't know," said Annette. "He's so—er—"

"I don't find him odd," said Rainborough, after waiting in vain for the epithet. "There's only one thing that's exceptional about Mischa,

the outside, this portrait suggests how exotic Canetti must seem to his English admirers. The artist who is also a polymath (or vice versa), and whose vocation is wisdom, is not a tradition which has a home in English, for all the numbers of bookish exiles from this century's more implacable tyrannies who have lugged their peerless learning, their unabashed projects of greatness, to the more modestly nourished English-speaking islands, large and small, off-shore of the European catastrophe.

Portraits drawn from the inside, with or without the poignant inflections of exile, have made familiar the model itinerant intellectual. He (for the type is male, of course) is a Jew, or like a Jew; polycultural, restless, misogynistic; a collector; dedicated to self-transcendence, despising the instincts; weighed down by books and buoyed up by the euphoria of knowledge. His real task is not to exercise his talent for explanation but, by being witness to the age, to set the largest, most *edifying* standards of despair. As a reclusive eccentric, he is one of the great achievements in life and letters of the twentieth century's imagination, a genuine hero, in the guise of a martyr. Although portraits of this figure have appeared in every European literature, some of the German ones have notable authority—*Steppenwolf*, certain essays by Walter Benjamin; or a notable

---

apart from his eyes, and that's his patience. He always has a hundred schemes on hand, and he's the only man I know who will wait literally for years for even a trivial plan to mature." Rainborough looked at Annette with hostility.

"Is it true that he cries over things he reads in the newspapers?" asked Annette.

"I should think it's most improbable!" said Rainborough. Annette's eyes were very wide . . .

The Flight from the Enchanter (Viking Press, 1956, p. 134)

bleakness—Canetti's one novel, *Auto-da-Fé*, and, recently, the novels of Thomas Bernhard, *Korrektur* [*Correction*] and *Der Weltverbesserer* [*The World Improver*].

Auto-da-Fé—the title in German is *Die Blendung* [*The Blinding*]—depicts the recluse as a book-besotted naïf who must undergo an epic of humiliation. The tranquilly celibate Professor Kien, a renowned Sinologist, is ensconced in his top-floor apartment with his twenty-five thousand books —books on all subjects, feeding a mind of unrelenting avidity. He does not know how horrible life is; will not know until he is separated from his books. Philistinism and mendacity appear in the form of a woman, ever the principle of anti-mind in this mythology of the intellectual: the reclusive scholar in the sky marries his housekeeper, a character as monstrous as any in the paintings of George Grosz or Otto Dix—and is pitched into the world.

Canetti relates that he first conceived *Auto-da-Fé*—he was twenty-four—as one of eight books, the main character of each to be a monomaniac and the whole cycle to be called "The Human Comedy of Madmen." But only the novel about "the bookman" (as Kien was called in early drafts), and not, say, the novels about the religious fanatic, the collector, or the technological visionary, got written. In the guise of a book about a lunatic—that is, as hyperbole— *Auto-da-Fé* purveys familiar clichés about unworldly, easily duped intellectuals and is animated by an exceptionally inventive hatred for women. It is impossible not to regard Kien's derangement as variations on his author's most cherished exaggerations. "The limitation to a particular, as though it were everything, is too despicable," Canetti noted—*The Human Province* is full of such Kien-like avowals. The author of the condescending remarks about women preserved in these notebooks might have enjoyed fabulating the details of Kien's delirious misogyny. And one can't help supposing that some of Canetti's work practices are evoked in the novel's account of a prodigious scholar plying his obsessional trade, afloat in a sea of manias and schemes of orderliness. Indeed, one would be surprised to learn that Canetti doesn't have a large, scholarly, but unspecialized library with the range of Kien's. This sort of library building has nothing to do with the book collecting that Benjamin memorably described, which is a passion for books as material objects (rare books, first editions). It is, rather, the materialization of an obsession whose ideal is to put the books inside one's head; the real library is only a mnemonic system. Thus Canetti has Kien sitting at his desk and composing a learned article without turning a single page of his books, except in his head.

Auto-da-Fé depicts the stages of Kien's madness as three relations of "head" and "world"—Kien secluded with his books as "a head without a world"; adrift in the bestial city, "a world without a head"; driven to suicide by "the world in the head." And this was not language suitable only for the mad bookman; Canetti later used it in his notebooks to describe himself, as when he called his life nothing but a desperate attempt to think about everything "so that it comes together in a head and thus becomes one again," affirming the very fantasy he had pilloried in *Auto-da-Fé*.

The heroic avidity thus described in his notebooks is the same goal Canetti had proclaimed at sixteen—"to learn everything"—for which, he relates in *The Tongue Set Free*, his mother denounced him as selfish and irresponsible. To covet, to thirst, to long for—these are passionate but also acquisitive relations to knowledge and truth;

Canetti recalls a time when, never without scruples, he "even invented elaborate excuses and rationales for having books." The more immature the avidity, the more radical the fantasies of throwing off the burden of books and learning. *Auto-da-Fé*, which ends with the bookman immolating himself with his books, is the earliest and crudest of these fantasies. Canetti's later writings project more wistful, prudent fantasies of disburdenment. A note from 1951: "His dream: to know everything he knows and yet not know it."

Published in 1935 to praise from Broch, Thomas Mann, and others, *Auto-da-Fé* was Canetti's first book (if one does not count a play he wrote in 1932) and only novel, the product of an enduring taste for hyperbole and a fascination with the grotesque that became in later works more static, considerably less apocalyptic. *Earwitness* (1974) is like an abstract distillation of the novel-cycle about lunatics Canetti conceived when he was in his twenties. This short book consists of rapid sketches of fifty forms of monomania, of "characters" such as the Corpse-Skulker, the Fun Runner, the Narrow-Smeller, the Misspeaker, the Woe Administrator; fifty characters and no plot. The ungainly names suggest an inordinate degree of self-consciousness about literary invention—for Canetti is a writer who endlessly questions, from the vantage of the moralist, the very possibility of making art. "If one knows a lot of people," he had noted years earlier, "it seems almost blasphemous to invent more."

A year after the publication of *Auto-da-Fé*, in his homage to Broch, Canetti cites Broch's stern formula: "Literature is always an impatience on the part of knowledge."

But Broch's gifts for patience were rich enough to produce those great, patient novels *The Death of Virgil* and *The Sleepwalkers*, and to inform a grandly speculative intelligence. Canetti worried about what could be done with the novel, which indicates the quality of his own impatience. For Canetti, to think is to insist; he is always offering himself choices, asserting and reasserting his *right* to do what he does. He chose to embark on what he calls a "life work," and disappeared for twenty-five years to hatch that work, publishing nothing after 1938, when he left Vienna (except for a second play), until 1960, when *Crowds and Power* appeared. "Everything," he says, went into this book.

Canetti's ideals of patience and his irrepressible feeling for the grotesque are united in his impressions of a trip to Morocco, *The Voices of Marrakesh* (1967). The book's vignettes of minimal survival present the grotesque as a form of heroism: a pathetic skeletal donkey with a huge erection; and the most wretched of beggars, blind children begging and, atrocious to imagine, a brown bundle emitting a single sound (*e-e-e-e-e*) which is brought every day to a square in Marrakesh to collect alms and to which Canetti pays a moving, characteristic tribute: "I was proud of the bundle because it was alive."

Humility is the theme of another work of this period, "Kafka's Other Trial," written in 1969, which treats Kafka's life as an exemplary fiction and offers a commentary on it. Canetti relates the drawn-out calamity of Kafka's engagement to Felice Bauer (Kafka's letters to Felice had just been published) as a parable about the secret victory of the one who chooses failure, who "withdraws from power in whatever form it might appear." He notes with admiration that Kafka often identifies with weak small animals, finding in Kafka his own feelings about the renunciation of power. In fact, in the force of his testimony to the ethical imperative of siding with the humiliated and the powerless, he seems closer to Simone Weil, another great expert on power, whom he never mentions. Canetti's identification with the powerless lies outside history, however; the epitome of powerlessness for Canetti is not, say, oppressed people but animals. Canetti, who is not a Christian, does not conceive of any intervention or active partisanship. Neither is he resigned. Incapable of insipidity or satiety, Canetti advances the model of a mind always reacting, registering shocks and trying to outwit them.

The aphoristic writing of his notebooks is fast knowledge—in contrast to the slow knowledge distilled in *Crowds and Power*. "My task," he wrote in 1949, a year after he began writing it, "is to show how complex selfishness is." For such a long book, it is very tense. His rapidity wars with his tenacity. The somewhat laborious, assertive writer who set out to write a tome that will "grab this century by the throat" interferes with, and is interfered with by, a concise writer who is more playful, more insolent, more puzzled, more scornful.

The notebook is the perfect literary form for an eternal student, someone who has no subject or, rather, whose subject is "everything." It allows entries of all lengths and shapes and degrees of impatience and roughness, but its ideal entry is the aphorism. Most of Canetti's entries take up the aphorist's traditional themes: the hypocrisies of society, the vanity of human wishes, the sham of love, the ironies of death, the pleasure and necessity of solitude, and the intricacies of one's own thought processes. Most of the great aphorists have been pessimists, purveyors of scorn for human folly. ("The great writers of aphorisms read as if they had all known each other well," Canetti has noted.) Aphoristic thinking is informal, unsociable, adversarial, proudly selfish. "One needs friends mainly in order to become impudent—that is, more oneself," Canetti writes: there is the authentic tone of the aphorist. The notebook holds that ideally impudent, efficient self that one constructs to deal with the world. By the disjunction of ideas and observations, by the brevity of their expression, by the absence of helpful illustration, the notebook makes of thinking something light.

Despite having much of the aphorist's temperament, Canetti is anything but an intellectual dandy. (He is the opposite of, say, Gottfried Benn.) Indeed, the great limit of Canetti's sensibility is the absence of the slightest trace of the aesthete. Canetti shows no love of art as such. He has his roster of Great Writers, but no painting, theater, film, dance, or the other familiars of humanist culture figure in his work. Canetti appears to stand rather grandly above the impacted ideas of "culture" or "art." He does not love anything the mind fabricates for its own sake. His writing, therefore, has little irony. No one touched by the aesthetic sensibility would have noted, severely, "What often bothers me about Montaigne is the fat on the quotations." There is nothing in Canetti's temperament that could respond to Surrealism, to speak only of the most persuasive modern option for the aesthete. Nor, it would seem, was he ever touched by the temptation of the left.

A dedicated enlightener, he describes the object of his struggle as the one faith left intact by the Enlightenment, "the most preposterous of all, the religion of power." Here is the side of Canetti that reminds one of Karl Kraus, for whom the ethical vocation is endless protest. But no writer is less a journalist than Canetti. To protest against power, power as such; to protest against death (he is one of the great death-haters of literature)—these are broad targets, rather invincible enemies. Canetti describes Kafka's work as a "refutation" of power, and this is Canetti's aim in *Crowds and Power*. All of his work, however, aims at a refutation of death. A refutation seems to mean for Canetti an inordinate insisting. Canetti insists that death is really unacceptable; unassimilable, because it is what is outside life; unjust, because it limits ambition and insults it. He refuses to understand death, as Hegel suggested, as something within life—as the *consciousness* of death, finitude, mortality. In matters of death Canetti is an unregenerate, appalled materialist, and unrelentingly quixotic. "I still haven't succeeded in doing anything against death," he wrote in 1960.

In *The Tongue Set Free* Canetti is eager to do justice to each of his admirations, which is a way of keeping someone alive. Typically, Canetti also means this literally. Displaying his usual unwillingness to be reconciled to extinction, Canetti recalls a teacher in boarding school and concludes: "In case he is still in the world today, at ninety or one hundred, I would like him to know I bow to him."

This first volume of his autobiography is dominated by the history of a profound admiration: that of Canetti for his mother. It is the portrait of one of the great teacher-parents, a zealot of European high culture self-confidently at work before the time that turned such a parent into a selfish tyrant and such a child into an "overachiever," to

WHAT DOES SHE BASE THIS ON?

use the philistine label which conveys the contemporary disdain for precocity and intellectual ardor.

"Mother, whose highest veneration was for great writers," was the primal admirer; and a passionate, merciless promoter of her admirations. Canetti's education consisted of immersion in books and their amplification in talk. There were evening readings aloud, tempestuous conversations about everything they read, about the writers they agreed to revere. Many discoveries were made separately, but they had to admire in unison, and a divergence was fought out in lacerating debates until one or the other yielded. His mother's policies of admiration created a tense world, defined by loyalties and betrayals. Each new admiration could throw one's life into question. Canetti describes his mother being distracted and exalted for a week after hearing the *St. Matthew Passion*, finally weeping because she fears that Bach has made her want only to listen to music and that "it's all over with books." Canetti, age thirteen, comforts her and reassures her that she *will* still want to read.

Witnessing his mother's leaps and raging contradictions of character "with amazement and admiration," Canetti does not underestimate her cruelty. Ominously enough, her favorite modern writer for a long time was Strindberg; in another generation it would probably have been D. H. Lawrence. Her emphasis on "character building" often led this fiercest of readers to berate her studious child for pursuing "dead knowledge," avoiding "hard" reality, letting books and conversation make him "unmanly." (She despised women, Canetti reports.) Canetti relates how annihilated by her he sometimes felt and then turns this into a liberation. As he affirmed in himself his mother's capacity for passionate commitment, he chose to revolt against the febrility of her enthusiasms, the overexclusiveness of her avidity. Patience ("monumental patience"), steadfastness, and universality of concern became his goals. His mother's world has no animals—only great men; Canetti will have both. She cares only about literature and hates science; starting in 1924 he will study chemistry at the University of Vienna, taking his Ph.D. in 1929. She scoffs at his interest in primitive peoples; Canetti will avow, as he prepares to write *Crowds and Power*: "It is a serious goal of my life to get to know all myths of all peoples."

Canetti refuses the victim's part. There is much chivalry in his portrait of his mother. It also reflects something like a policy of triumphalism—a steadfast refusal of tragedy, of irremediable suffering, that seems related to his refusal of finitude, of death, and from which comes much of Canetti's energy: his staunchless capacity for admiration and enthusiasm, and his civilized contempt for complaining.

Canetti's mother was undemonstrative—the slightest caress was an event. But her talk—debating, hectoring, musing, recounting her life—was lavish, torrential. Language was the medium of their passion: words and more words. With language Canetti made his "first independent move" from his mother: learning Swiss German (she hated "vulgar" dialects) when he went away to boarding school at fourteen. And with language he remained connected to her: writing a five-act verse tragedy in Latin (with an interlinear German translation for her benefit, it filled 121 pages), which he dedicated to her and sent, requesting from her a detailed commentary.

Canetti seems eager to enumerate the many skills which he owes to his mother's example and teaching—including

/ 194

those which he developed to oppose her, also generously counted as her gifts: obstinacy, intellectual independence, rapidity of thought. He also speculates that the liveliness of Ladino, which he'd spoken as a child, helped him to think fast. (For the precocious, thinking is a kind of speed.) Canetti gives a complex account of that extraordinary process which learning is for an intellectually precocious child —fuller and more instructive than the accounts in, say, Mill's *Autobiography* or Sartre's *The Words*. For Canetti's capacities as an admirer reflect tireless skills as a learner; the first cannot be deep without the second. As an exceptional learner, Canetti has an irrepressible loyalty to teachers, to what they do well even (or especially when) they do it inadvertently. The teacher at his boarding school to whom he now "bows" won his fealty by being brutal during a class visit to a slaughterhouse. Forced by him to confront a particularly gruesome sight, Canetti learned that the murder of animals was something "I wasn't meant to get over." His mother, even when she was brutal, was always feeding his flagrant alertness with her words. Canetti says proudly, "I find mute knowledge dangerous."

Canetti claims to be a "hear-er" rather than a "see-er." In *Auto-da-Fé*, Kien practices being blind, for he has discovered that "blindness is a weapon against time and space; our being is one vast blindness." Particularly in his work since *Crowds and Power*—such as the didactically titled *The Voices of Marrakesh*, *Earwitness*, *The Tongue Set Free* —Canetti stresses the moralist's organ, the ear, and slights the eye (continuing to ring changes on the theme of blindness). Hearing, speaking, and breathing are praised whenever something important is at stake, if only in the form of

ear, mouth (or tongue), and throat metaphors. When Canetti observes that "the *loudest* passage in Kafka's work
tells of this guilt with respect to the animals," the adjective
is itself a form of insistence.

What is heard is voices—to which the ear is a witness.
(Canetti does not talk about music, nor indeed about any
art that is non-verbal.) The ear is the attentive sense,
humbler, more passive, more immediate, less discriminat-
ing than the eye. Canetti's disavowal of the eye is an aspect
of his remoteness from the aesthete's sensibility, which typically affirms the pleasures and the wisdom of the visual;
that is, of surfaces. To give sovereignty to the ear is an
obtrusive, consciously archaizing theme in Canetti's later
work. Implicitly he is restating the archaic gap between
Hebrew as opposed to Greek culture, ear culture as opposed to eye culture, and the moral versus the aesthetic.

Canetti equates knowing with hearing, and hearing with
hearing everything and still being able to respond. The
exotic impressions garnered during his stay in Marrakesh
are unified by the quality of attentiveness to "voices" that
Canetti tries to summon in himself. Attentiveness is the
formal subject of the book. Encountering poverty, misery,
and deformity, Canetti undertakes to hear, that is, really to
pay attention to words, cries, and inarticulate sounds "on
the edge of the living." His essay on Kraus portrays someone whom Canetti considers ideal both as hearer and as
voice. Canetti says that Kraus was haunted by voices; that
his ear was constantly open; that "the real Karl Kraus was
the *speaker*." Describing a writer as a voice has become
such a cliché that it is possible to miss the force—and the
characteristic literalness—of what Canetti means. The voice
for Canetti stands for irrefutable presence. To treat some-

one as a voice is to grant authority to that person; to affirm that one hears means that one hears what must be heard.

Like a scholar in a Borges story that mixes real and imaginary erudition, Canetti has a taste for fanciful blends of knowledge, eccentric classifications, and spirited shifts of tone. Thus *Crowds and Power*—in German, *Masse und Macht*—offers analogies from physiology and zoology to explain command and obedience; and is perhaps most original when it extends the notion of the crowd to include collective units, not composed of human beings, which "recall" the crowd, are "felt to be a crowd," which "stand as a symbol for it in myth, dream, speech, and song." (Among such units—in Canetti's ingenious catalogue—are fire, rain, the fingers of the hand, the bee swarm, teeth, the forest, the snakes of delirium tremens.) Much of *Crowds and Power* depends on latent or inadvertent science-fiction imagery of things, or parts of things, that become eerily autonomous; of unpredictable movements, tempos, volumes. Canetti turns time (history) into space, in which a weird array of biomorphic entities—the various forms of the Great Beast, the Crowd—disport themselves. The crowd moves, emits, grows, expands, contracts. Its options come in pairs: crowds are said by Canetti to be quick and slow, rhythmic and stagnant, closed and open. The pack (another version of the crowd) laments, it preys, it is tranquil, it is outward or inward.

As an account of the psychology and structure of authority, *Crowds and Power* harks back to nineteenth-century talk about crowds and masses in order to expound its poetics of political nightmare. Condemnation of the French Revolution, and later of the Commune, was the message of the nineteenth-century books on crowds (they were as common then as they are unfashionable now), from Charles Mackay's *Extraordinary Popular Delusions and the Madness of Crowds* (1841) to Le Bon's *The Crowd* (1895), a book Freud admired, and *The Psychology of Revolution* (1912). But whereas earlier writers had been content to assert the crowd's pathology and moralize about it, Canetti means to explain, explain exhaustively, for example, the crowd's destructiveness ("often mentioned as its most conspicuous quality," he says) with his biomorphic paradigms. And unlike Le Bon, who was making a case against revolution and for the status quo (considered by Le Bon the less oppressive dictatorship), Canetti offers a brief against power itself.

To understand power by considering the crowd, to the detriment of notions like "class" or "nation," is precisely to insist on an ahistorical understanding. Hegel and Marx are not mentioned, not because Canetti is so self-confident that he won't deign to drop the usual names, but because the implications of Canetti's argument are sharply anti-Hegelian and anti-Marxist. His ahistorical method and conservative political temper bring Canetti rather close to Freud —though he is in no sense a Freudian. Canetti is what Freud might have been were he *not* a psychologist: using many sources that were important to Freud—the autobiography of the psychotic Judge Schreber, material on anthropology and the history of ancient religions, Le Bon's crowd theory—he comes to quite different conclusions about group psychology and the shaping of the ego. Like Freud, Canetti tends to find the prototype of crowd (that is, irrational) behavior in religion, and much of *Crowds and Power* is really a rationalist's discourse about religion. For example,

what Canetti calls the lamenting pack is just another name
for religions of lament, of which he gives a dazzling analysis, contrasting the slow tempos of Catholic piety and ritual
(expressing the Church's perennial fear of the open crowd)
with the frenzied mourning in the Shi'ite branch of Islam.

Like Freud, too, Canetti dissolves politics into pathology, treating society as a mental activity—a barbaric one,
of course—that must be decoded. Thus he moves, without
breaking stride, from the notion of the crowd to the
"crowd symbol," and analyzes social grouping and the
forms of community as transactions of crowd symbols.
Some final turn of the crowd argument seems to have been
reached when Canetti puts the French Revolution in its
place, finding the Revolution less interesting as an eruption
of the destructive than as a "national crowd symbol" for the
French.

For Hegel and his successors, the historical (the home of
irony) and the natural are two radically different processes. In *Crowds and Power*, history is "natural." Canetti
argues to history, not from it. First comes the account of
the crowd; then, as illustration, the section called "The
Crowd in History." History is used only to furnish examples
—a rapid use. Canetti is partial to the evidence of history-
less (in the Hegelian sense) peoples, treating anthropological anecdotes as having the same illustrative value as an
event taking place in an advanced historical society.

Crowds and Power is an eccentric book—made literally
eccentric by its ideal of "universality," which leads Canetti
to avoid making the obvious reference: Hitler. He appears indirectly, in the central importance Canetti gives to
the case of Judge Schreber. (Here is Canetti's only reference to Freud—in one discreet footnote, where Canetti says

that had Freud lived a bit longer he might have seen Schreber's paranoid delusions in a more pertinent way: as a prototype of the political, specifically Nazi, mentality.) But Canetti is genuinely not Eurocentric—one of his large achievements as a mind. Conversant with Chinese as well as European thought, with Buddhism and Islam as well as Christianity, Canetti enjoys a remarkable freedom from reductive habits of thinking. He seems incapable of using psychological knowledge in a reductive way; the author of the homage to Broch could not have been thinking about anything as ordinary as personal motives. And he fights the more plausible reduction to the historical. "I would give a great deal to get rid of my habit of seeing the world historically," he wrote in 1950, two years after he started writing *Crowds and Power*.

His protest against seeing historically is directed not just against that most plausible of reductionisms. It is also a protest against death. To think about history is to think about the dead; and to be incessantly reminded that one is mortal. Canetti's thought is conservative in the most literal sense. It—he—does not want to die.

"I want to feel everything in me before I think it," Canetti wrote in 1943, and for this, he says, he needs a long life. To die prematurely means having not fully engorged himself and, therefore, having not used his mind as he could. It is almost as if Canetti had to keep his consciousness in a permanent state of avidity, to remain unreconciled to death. "It is wonderful that nothing is lost in a mind," he also wrote in his notebook, in what must have been a not infrequent moment of euphoria, "and would not this alone be reason enough to live very long or even forever?" Recurrent images of needing to feel everything inside himself, of unifying everything in one head, illustrate Canetti's attempts through magical thinking and moral clamorousness to "refute" death.

Canetti offers to strike a bargain with death. "A century? A paltry hundred years! Is that too much for an earnest intention!" But why one hundred years? Why not three hundred?—like the 337-year-old heroine of Karel Čapek's *The Makropulos Affair* (1922). In the play, one character (a socialist "progressive") describes the disadvantages of a normal life span.

> What can a man do during his sixty years of life?
> What enjoyment has he? What can he learn? You
> don't live to get the fruit of the tree you have
> planted; you'll never learn all the things that man-
> kind has discovered before you; you won't com-
> plete your work or leave your example behind you;
> you'll die without having even lived. A life of three
> hundred years on the other hand would allow fifty
> years to be a child and a pupil; fifty years to get to
> know the world and see all that exists in it; one hun-
> dred years to work for the benefit of all; and then,
> when he has achieved all human experience, another
> hundred years to live in wisdom, to rule, to teach,
> and to set an example. Oh, how valuable human life
> would be if it lasted three hundred years.

He sounds like Canetti—except that Canetti does not justify his yearning for longevity with any appeal to its greater scope for good works. So large is the value of the mind that it alone is used to oppose death. Because the mind is so real to him Canetti dares to challenge death, and because the body is so unreal he perceives nothing dismaying about extreme longevity. Canetti is more than willing to live as a centenarian; he does not, while he is fantasizing, ask for what Faust demanded, the return of youth, or for what Emilia Makropulos was given by her alchemist father, its magical prolongation. Youth has no part in Canetti's fantasy of immortality. It is pure longevity, the longevity of the mind. It is simply assumed that character has the same stake as mind in longevity: Canetti thought "the brevity of life makes us bad." Emilia Makropulos suggests its longevity would make us worse:

> You cannot go on loving for three hundred years. And you cannot go on hoping, creating, gazing at things for three hundred years. You can't stand it. Everything becomes boring. It's boring to be good and boring to be bad. . . . And then you realize that nothing actually exists. . . . You are so close to everything. You can see some point in everything. For you everything has some value because those few years of yours won't be enough to satisfy your enjoyment. . . . It's disgusting to think how happy you are. And it's simply due to the ridiculous coincidence that you're going to die soon. You take an ape-like interest in everything. . . .

But this plausible doom is just what Canetti cannot admit. He is unperturbed by the possibility of the flagging of appetite, the satiation of desire, the devaluation of passion. Canetti gives no thought to the decomposition of the feelings any more than of the body, only to the persistence of the mind. Rarely has anyone been so at home in the mind, with so little ambivalence.

Canetti is someone who has felt in a profound way the responsibility of words, and much of his work makes the effort to communicate something of what he has learned about how to pay attention to the world. There is no doctrine, but there is a great deal of scorn, urgency, grief, and euphoria. The message of the mind's passions is passion. "I try to imagine someone saying to Shakespeare, 'Relax!' " says Canetti. His work eloquently defends tension, exertion, moral and amoral seriousness.

But Canetti is not just another hero of the will. Hence the unexpected last attribute of a great writer that he finds in Broch: such a writer, he says, teaches us how to breathe. Canetti commends Broch's writings for their "rich store of breathing experience." It was Canetti's deepest, oddest compliment, and therefore one he also paid to Goethe (the most predictable of his admirations): Canetti also reads Goethe as saying, "Breathe!" Breathing may be the most radical of occupations, when construed as a liberation from other needs such as having a career, building a reputation, accumulating knowledge. What Canetti says at the end of this progress of admiration, his homage to Broch, suggests what there is most to admire. The last achievement of the serious admirer is to stop immediately putting to work the energies aroused by, filling up the space opened by, what is admired. Thereby talented admirers give themselves permission to breathe, to breathe more deeply. But for that it is necessary to go beyond avidity; to identify with something beyond achievement, beyond the gathering of power.

(1980)

ABOUT THE AUTHOR

SUSAN SONTAG is the author of two novels, *The Benefactor* and *Death Kit*, and a collection of short stories, *I, etcetera*. Her other books include *Against Interpretation*, *Trip to Hanoi*, *Styles of Radical Will*, *On Photography* (winner of the National Book Critics Circle Award for Criticism) and *Illness as Metaphor*.